LATIN AMERICA
ON BICYCLE

THE AUTHORS

JEAN-PIERRE PANET is an environmental engineer. When his work takes him to the subarctic near Hudson's Bay, or to the wilds along a major urban expressway, his bicycle is usually close at hand.

PAUL GLASSMAN, "one of the best-known authors on Central America" (according to *Library Journal*), has written and collaborated on a number of travel-related books.

LATIN AMERICA ON BICYCLE

BY
JEAN-PIERRE PANET
WITH
PAUL GLASSMAN

PASSPORT PRESS

ISBN 0-930016-27-0

Published and distributed by:

Passport Press
Box 1346
Champlain, New York 12919

e-mail: travelbook@yahoo.com

PRINTED IN THE UNITED STATES OF AMERICA

CONTENTS

1
INTRODUCTION

First, let me tell you a couple of things about myself. I am an environmental engineer and something of an ecologist. For me, bicycling is an economical and ecologically sound way to travel. If more people got around by bicycle, our cities would be less polluted, we'd all be healthier, and I think we'd all be happier.

Enough said.

Because you don't have to be an ecologist to discover Latin America on bicycle. An average interest in your surroundings, a normal ability to appreciate the sounds and scents of people and scenery up close, are all you need.

Nor do you have to be an adventurer or an intrepid explorer. But if you are going to ride a bicycle through exotic lands, you should have a minimally practical turn of mind. Good preparation will help, as will a flair for the unusual, and an ability to deal with the unexpected. Also, you should be open-minded.

Nor do you have to be an athlete. You can take most of the trips I'll describe if you are in good enough shape for a weekend bicycle outing.

You don't have to be excessively thrifty to pedal your way through Latin America. Personally, I like to sleep well and in moderate comfort after a day on my two wheels, and to dine on good food, when I can find it. But I'll also put up with beans and a hard bed. However, if you combine your cycling with camping, and cooking local foods for yourself, your cost can be practically nothing.

Nor do you have to be a linguist. Though you will be away from guides and interpreters, you can manage quite well with a limited, practical vocabulary.

You don't have to be very serious. In fact, a sense of humor would help.

Latin America is many things: a huge area of startling contrasts of wealth and poverty, of hope and despair, of breakneck progress and entrenched tradition, of trackless jungles and elegant cities. There are mountains that brush the sky, plants and animals that exist nowhere else, torrid and temperate and frigid climates, and great expanses of sandy beach.

Latin America is home to the largest numbers of Spanish- and Portuguese-speakers in the world, to more Catholics than anywhere else, to civilizations that achieved scientific discoveries while Europe was still in the dark ages, and which are struggling still to adapt to a modern world.

Latin America is also one great cycling path.

Latin America is much else, of course, but let me pause for a moment and tell you about the cycling path.

You see, Latin America is more developed than most areas of what's now called the Third World. The countries "down there" have fairly well developed road systems—not up to those of North America or Europe, but at least the roads exist. However, private car ownership is still not the norm in the countries to the south. So people and goods move in buses and trucks, and only sometimes in cars. And the right of way is usually wide open for the cyclist.

So the possibility of cycling is there. But let me say why cycling is a practical and even a desirable way to go.

The temperature and climate are suitable for biking all year. Not everywhere, of course. But in most countries, there are few extremes of cold, except at high altitudes. And you can plan for climate with near certainty. If it's the rainy season, it will rain every day, and of course you'll stay away. In the dry season, it rains never . . . or hardly ever. There is a suitable destination—a destination where conditions are, indeed, perfection—at any time of year.

There are few better ways than biking to thoroughly discover a country and use all of your time to advantage. If you go by another means, say, by bus, the time you spend is usually a negative part of your trip. You lose time waiting for a bus. The bus itself is possibly in bad mechanical condition, dangerous on mountain roads as well as uncomfortable and noisy, partially isolating you from your surroundings.

If you go by car, renting a vehicle can be very expensive. You could be at the mercy of greedy officials. There will be places you will not be able to go in some types of vehicles. In your own car, you may well dread having a breakdown far from home, but near dishonest mechanics.

On an organized tour, you may get to see exactly what you want to see. But then again, you may get to see nothing.

I don't want to discredit other means of transportation. They have their benefits for many travellers, including, from time to time, for me. I take buses and trains myself to avoid retracing a route, or when the terrain is too tough. But I want to concentrate on the positive aspects of bicycling relative to other ways of getting around.

The time you spend getting from place to place on a bicycle is positive time, not lost time. You not only see things, you feel them, you hear them, you live them up close. You smell the flowers and also the stenches, you feel the warmth of the sun and the damp chill of the mountains, you know the terrain because when it's going up and down you are dealing with it, it is part of what your trip is about.

You see things that you would never see otherwise, things that you would not be able to stop for when travelling on a bus or in a car or in a plane. In cities, where most tourists end up spending most of their time, things look basically the same. On bicycle, you get into the countryside, where you really note differences in countries, in peoples, in how they live.

By travelling under your own power, you appreciate more the nature of things: why a village is located in a certain place, near water or where people can bring their goods to market; how the face of the land has been changed by humans; how the soil and climate affect the crops grown in different places. There are more sophisticated ways to find these things out, but on a bicycle you sense them, too.

You maintain your shape, instead of being led around and accumulating flab. You won't have to diet or otherwise compensate for your trip when you get home.

You're independent. You don't depend on bus schedules. You don't depend on cars. You depend on yourself.

You find suitable accommodations more easily. You can visit half a dozen hotels in 30 minutes by bicycle, with no parking problems. You won't be stuck at the flophouse where the bus parks. If a good hotel is six kilometers out of town, you'll get there in half an hour by bicycle and have fun on the way.

You show a different face to the local people, and elicit reactions that your countrymen would never encounter. You see, in Latin America, white people travel down the road in Mercedes, or huge pickup trucks, or in escorted tour groups. The simple people are used to seeing these outsiders—their countrymen and others—and not talking with them. They see tourists and say "gringo, gringo" for lack of any real knowledge of you, or you of them. But when you travel on bicycle they cannot say anything. You travel among them, you on your bicycle, they on foot or by bus. They respect you, they see you and treat you as a human. It hasn't happened very often that people called out "gringo" as we passed. Usually it's the opposite. They come over, they see that you are very different, they talk to you, not at you.

It's exciting, exotic, different, a special experience when you go by bicycle. You may never climb Everest, or reach the North Pole. But how many of your friends have reached Chichicastenango on two wheels?

Also, it's fun. Especially going downhill.

There are some myths about bicycling far from home. People ask: Aren't you afraid of being robbed on the roads? Well, not more than here. Not more than anywhere else. In fact, what happens is that nobody looks upon you as a likely victim. You don't exactly look poor, but you don't look well off, at least to locals, because even poor people can pay for the bus. So they have a certain respect for you.

Another misconception is that bicycle travel is difficult. Maybe 90 percent of the time it is as easy as riding around in the city. When the going gets tough, you can always flag down a bus. After all, you're not in the middle of nowhere, or even in Los Angeles. Buses run everywhere in Latin America.

Nor is cycling in Latin America dangerous. Out in the countryside, you're less likely to be hit by a car than in town, where there are thousands of cars. Drivers in Latin America are used to finding things along or in the road: horses, oxcarts, people, stalled vehicles, even bicycles. I don't mean that you're sure of not having an accident. But the chances are lower than here. Drivers don't treat you as if you don't have the right to exist.

I got started biking in Latin America because . . . well, perhaps for the same reasons that you picked up this book. I had taken some bicycle trips near my home in Montreal, in Vermont and New York State, I had hiked in the Canadian west and California and Alaska and in the Eastern U.S., I had been to Mexico numerous times, and in several European countries and Morocco on bicycle. I wanted something different. The four corners of the earth had been explored, but not in every way. My attention turned to Latin America, the logic said yes, and it turned out to be . . . read ahead, and you'll see.

This is not a guide to all countries in Latin America, and all the cycling routes therein. Nor is it even a guide to the best routes. I haven't ridden them all, not yet. But I want to tell you about the places I've been and how it was to go on bicycle. I'll tell you what went well, and where I made mistakes. Use my experiences and re-trace my routes, or blaze your own trails.

But first, I'll tell you what equipment you need to take for any cycling trip in Latin America, and the practical preparations you need to make. I'll also give you some general advice about day-to-day routines on the road.

Let's go.

2
WHAT TO TAKE

YOUR BICYCLE

I recommend that you use a strong, solid bike designed for touring. You may or may not cover long distances, you may or may not face challenging terrain, you may or may not be hard on your bicycle. But for sure you will be carrying more baggage than on day outings. You don't want your means of transport to fall apart far from home in the middle of your adventure.

There are many kinds of touring bike to choose from, and new ones are continually coming on the market.

Your bicycle should have a minimum of ten or twelve speeds. To deal with the more difficult ascents, fifteen- or eighteen-speed bikes are really desirable. Their extra Alpine gears give your knees a break and make long ascents easy and fun.

In broad terms, you have a choice between a **mountain bike** and a traditional **touring bike**. I've taken trips on both kinds. I've mostly used an eighteen-speed touring bike, which I've found more than adequate, even on gravel roads. I've also used a mountain bike with good results. Here are the comparisons:

Weight: Less for a touring bike. A mountain bike is several pounds heavier, a negative factor.

Gearing: Pedalling is generally a bit more easy in the lowest speed on a mountain bike. Sometimes you can face a grade of as much as ten percent, and that little bit is important.

Sturdiness: A mountain bike has all the advantage. Though I've never had serious problems in this respect, I've sometimes ridden delicately or walked a touring bike to avoid damage on rough stretches. But everything is bigger and more heavy-duty on a mountain bike. Which also means it will survive an airplane trip better.

Tires: You can get tough, puncture-resistant Kevlar tires for a touring bike. But on a good mountain bike, with big, thick tires, the risk of flats is virtually nil. There is more rolling resistance on a mountain bike, however.

Off-road stability: much greater on a mountain bike.

Speed on paved road: faster on a touring bike.

Speed on gravel roads: slightly faster on a mountain bike.

Comfort: about the same on paved roads. On a gravel road, better on a mountain bike.

Luggage facility: Equivalent on both.

WHICH BIKE FOR YOU?

To sum up: If speed over long distances is not your main criterion, a mountain-type bicycle is more likely to fulfill your needs. But this is a broad statement. Much depends on the type of biking you will be doing, and the bike that feels right for you. The is no one bike that is perfect for everybody, but everybody can find a suitable bike.

A typical mountain bike can use some **adaptations to its standard equipment**, in the way of pedals, fenders, seats and carriers. And by mountain-type bike, I don't necessarily mean the cheapened model you'll find in department stores for less than $150. These are inferior machines with unsturdy frames and bottom-of-the-line accessories. You would be very lucky (and I would be very surprised) if something didn't break on one of these within a short time.

Also, don't just buy a bike, even the best 18-speed touring bike, and go off on a trip with it. I have a friend who did just that, and he was miserable. The saddle chafed, he was constantly making adjustments as the gear cables wore in. If you have a 12-speed touring bike and you're used to it, take it! More than any hard and fast rules, **you want a bike you're comfortable with**. Best not to attempt breaking in a strange bicycle in a strange environment. If you buy a bike with a long trip in mind, the thing to do is to take some weekend trips first, so you and the bike can get on friendly terms with each other.

For similar reasons, **never plan to rent a bike**. Always bring your own. First of all, you will never find a bike that is the quality of your own. And you will not be comfortable. Once I rented a bike in Mexico. After two hours, I had the feeling of sitting on a fakir's seat—a lot of pain. Many people are amazed that I bring my own bike, but it's the only way.

HOW TO EQUIP YOUR BIKE

There are books and books on equipment and accessories, and these, and bicycle shops, will give you good counsel. But I will add a few recommendations of my own.

Handlebars

I prefer straight, town-type handlebars. These allow a more upright position when riding, which gives you a better field of vision. Your brakes are close at hand, which is useful for when you have to brake for hours, as when going down a volcano or from a mountain pass. You have to apply less effort, and you can brake more quickly and effectively. But others are used to lower, racing-type handlebars, and prefer these for touring.

Tires

It's important for your tires to make good contact with the road surface. On a touring bike, use the widest tire you can fit on your frame, generally an inch and a quarter or an inch and three eighths, made of Kevlar. To use a mountain bike for touring, leave your standard mountain-bike tire at home, and replace it with one with a less-aggressive tread, to increase your efficiency on a paved surface.

The saddle

The saddle is the most important part, the place where your body most consistently contacts machine. Usually—it's not a rule—your saddle is made of leather. With time, the leather will assume the form of your rear. Plastic will not. You must be perfectly comfortable with your saddle. If you're not, after two days, your trip is finished. Only a well-broken-in saddle will do.

There are all sorts of saddles, men's and women's saddles, saddles padded with felt and with other materials. Personally, I'm happier on a woman's saddle. Many male friends agree. Women's saddles are slightly wider, and they're especially more comfortable if you're thin. In any case, within a few minutes of using it, you'll know if your saddle is right. If it's wrong, you'll have nothing but problems.

Many mountain bikes come with a quick-release clamp for adjusting or removing the saddle. My advice is to change it for a regular screw. You probably won't have to adjust your saddle when you're on tour, and the quick-release feature will only help a thief.

Lights

As for headlights, let me say first that you should never be on the road at night in a foreign country. You don't know what road conditions are or what you will encounter. But you're likely to be overtaken by nightfall at one time or another, so just for security you should bring a light. Take one that you can mount on your bike and use by hand as well. One that you just tape on when you need it will do.

Pedals

You might have to use different pedals from the ones that come with your bike. The new, flat pedals are comfortable if you don't wear biking shoes. I prefer them. A toe clip is important to increase your pedalling efficiency.

Reflectors

You should have front and rear and wheel-mounted reflectors.

Horn

A horn is not indispensable. You don't often have to beep, and yelling is just as effective.

Racks

Your carrier for your bike bag is important. Vibrations, especially on gravel roads, will eventually crack aluminum supports, which can't be welded in most countries. One good brand of rack is made by the Jim Blackburn company of California. On the front, you should have a low-ride rack. I try to rest about 35 percent of my luggage weight on the front, the remainder over the rear wheels. You might be more comfortable with a different distribution. Balance your weight evenly over your handlebars and over the rear wheels, otherwise you'll ride cockeyed. Never wear a backpack when riding. It's the wrong tool for the job. Even with a light load, it will become painful after a short time.

Bags

Your bike bags do not have to be too large, if you are selective about what you take. And certainly they should not to too wide, as you want to be able to squeeze through tight spots. Put some reflectors on your bags.

Many people prefer bike bags with outside pockets, for the convenience of having access to certain items quickly. That's fine, but just remember that if your bike is ever unguarded, a thief can easily get those same items as well.

Brakes
Cantilever brakes are recommended. They are simpler and more easily repaired than other types, and stronger and more easily adjustable.

Mirrors
You need a handlebar mirror. I think it's an important security device. Don't forget to take it off when you put your bicycle on the plane, otherwise it will break for sure and you'll have seven years of bad luck. There are other types of mirrors for your helmet. They're very good, once you get used to them.

Fenders
Plastic fenders will protect you and your bike to some degree from rain and gravel. And even if you're travelling at a dry time, there may be contaminated stagnant water in the streets. Fenders will keep coliform bacteria from splashing in your face.

Bottles
For many trips we have brought water bottles that attach to the bicycle. These are good for races, but for cross-country travel, you need a lot more water than these will ever hold. So I usually buy a large, sealed, plastic container of purified water and carry it in my bicycle bag. A collapsible large bottle of the type used in North America, which you fill when you find clean running water, is useless in most of Latin America—it collects algae after a few days.

License Plates

It helps to have a license plate on your bicycle. This is what many local authorities are used to. Anything that looks like a license plate will do—a university permit, a municipal registration—as long as it has a number. Customs officials, police at checkpoints, even your hotel clerk may note your number. It makes them happy, and saves you much explanation.

In general, **don't attach anything too high-tech to your bicycle**. If it breaks, you probably won't be able to fix it. Think of your bike as a pickup truck or a plain sedan, rather than as a fancy sports car. It may not get you there in style, but it will get you there.

WHAT TO CARRY

PACKING PRINCIPLES

Here are three rules:

• Don't forget anything you really need. Even if you can find a part or tool in the country you're travelling in, you could waste a lot of time looking for it.

• The less you have, the happier you will be.

• When you have everything you need, you should still have space left over, because luggage tends to increase as your trip progresses.

With these rules in mind, you should be able to prepare well for your trip.

Everything I carry fits in two small packs over the rear wheel, if I don't take camping equipment. I start with two front bags empty. And as needed, I put into them food, water, maps and books. This allows room for expansion of my goods as I go along.

I take pretty well the same things no matter where I go—the same emergency goods, tool kit, spare parts, first-aid equipment, and clothing. No matter where you go on a bicycle, you can have the same problems and needs, and as Murphy's Law stipulates, if you don't bring it, it will happen.

FIRST AID KIT

I'll talk more about first aid and medical concerns down the road. But for now, let me note that your first aid kit should include **Halazone** to disinfect water; a **malaria preventative** if indicated; **sun cream** with PABA; **aspirin** or other pain-relief tablets; **sterile pads**; **adhesive tape**; **bandages**; **mosquito repellent**; and any **medications** that you regularly take.

TOOL KIT

Let me take apart my tool kit and tell you what's in it. But first I'll remind you that you'll be on roads, which you share with cars, which often carry tools, which can be used in many cases on bicycles. And garages as well have many of the tools you'll need for minor or emergency repairs. And people in houses have tools. So there are a lot of tools that you do not absolutely have to bring for abstruse emergencies. You can't count on borrowing tools, but a friendly attitude will aid your request.

Here's what I have:

Brass wire (picture-frame wire). It can be used to repair anything—to hold fenders together, to keep equipment attached when you don't have the right screw, etc.

A **needle and thread**. Since you don't carry a lot of clothes, you need to repair those you do have if they rip. Also to repair bike bags, tent, etc.

Large **diaper pins**—also for repairs. These will replace a broken zipper.

A **compass**—to determine your direction. A small GPS device (Global Positioning System) could also come in handy.

A disposable **cigarette lighter**, as well as matches. To light your stove, candles, etc.

A couple of long-burning **candles**—good for extended blackouts. You don't want to run down your flashlight batteries.

Wheel spokes—make sure you have the right ones for your wheel. You can travel with one missing spoke, but with a couple gone, you'll find that they break one after another. Take two or three, and a spoke wrench for making adjustments.

You need a good **tire-pressure gauge** as well—one will do if there are several of you. When you sit on your bike and add your equipment, you're putting a lot of weight on your bike. It helps to be able to measure pressure accurately so that you don't stress your wheels. With 20 pounds of air, a tire can look to be adequately inflated, when it isn't.

A rubber patch kit.

One **inner tube** for a mountain bike, two for a touring bike. When the road surface is very hot, a rubber patch may not hold. It's better to change the tube, patch the damaged one, and put it away.

One **spare tire** for a touring bike. You probably won't need one for a mountain bike. The tire you take for a touring bike can be of normal city thickness. Fold it up, tape it, and stuff it into your baggage. Of course, replace well-used tires before you start your trip. Tires have a way of looking fine for a long time, and then suddenly giving up.

Plastic tools to take tires off rims (tire "irons").

A **tool to remove chain links** is essential. It will accomplish in seconds what could take you hours with a screwdriver or improvised tools. Though chain links break rarely, you can't count on them not breaking.

Spare **screws and nuts** to hold your accessories onto your bike. With vibrations, screws loosen and fall, and you'll never find them. Take spares for the screws and bolts that hold your mudguards, racks, and anything else.

A spare brake/gear cable.

A spare **brake pad**. If one of yours works loose and falls into a canyon, it's better not to waste time looking for it.

I always bring a **freewheel cog remover**. It's a small part that enables you to dismantle your back wheel, which you use in combination with a large wrench that you'll find in a garage. You'll use this in case of a major accident, and to change spokes on the side of your freewheel, but it's not really essential. A single missing spoke on that side can usually be left alone.

A **wrench** to remove your pedal—also not essential.

I take a Zefal-hp high-pressure **pump**. A high-pressure pump is required if your tires take 90 pounds of pressure, a standard pump for up to 45 pounds of pressure on a mountain bike. The Zefal comes with a set of adaptors for different valves—quite useful if you have to buy an inner-tube with a Presta valve instead of the Schrader valve used in North America.

Hexagonal **Allen-type wrenches** to fit your accessories. These get frequent use, so buy some of good quality.

A small **file**—useful for adjusting cantilever brakes.

A small jar of white bicycle grease.

A **wrench** to remove the bolt that fixes your front gear wheels—not mandatory.

An adjustable wrench.

A good **screwdriver** with interchangeable bits.

Oil for your chain. Keep the container in a plastic bag.

Two pairs of **pliers** to hold nuts.

All this fits in one pouch, except for the pump, which mounts on my bicycle.

CLOTHING

I've found that no matter where I've gone in Latin America, I've packed pretty well the same items of clothing. As far as temperature goes, you can usually forget about seasonal variations. Instead, you'll have to deal with climates that vary according to altitude. When you climb into the mountains, you'll reach temperatures near or even below freezing. Down at sea level, it could be sweltering, in the mid 30s Centigrade (90s Fahrenheit) at any time of year. Your clothing and gear must deal with all extremes.

All of my clothing goes in one of my rear bags, with a slight spillover into the other bag.

Shorts and **t-shirts** are my basic clothing, since it's sunny and warm most of the time (if I've planned things correctly). Two pairs of each will do. If you wish, you can use **biking shorts**, which don't ride up or chafe as you pedal. I wear regular **running shoes**, but many people insist on **biking shoes**. A good brand is Avocet. The rest of my clothing follows the onion model—layers that can be put on or peeled off as needed. Included should be one good woolen **sweater**, which will stay warm even when wet; three or four pairs of **socks**—I use cotton, but wool would do; two or three pairs of **underwear**—you'll be washing them each day; one pair of long pants; a **tuque** (woolen hat) or some other kind of warm headwear; and a **windbreaker**, or anorak, to go over everything else.   Mine is a cotton-nylon blend, which breathes. A **nylon shell** can go under the anorak to stop the wind in extremely cold conditions. A **hand towel** will do double duty as a scarf. A very good **raincoat**, and **rainpants**, are essential. Mine are Peterstorm brand, with hermetically sealed seams—I've seen rain pour through some others—and have come in useful even in the desert. No matter how warm it is, if you get wet through to the skin you'll be very cold, especially if there is any wind, and you won't be able to continue biking. With a good raincoat, you can travel all day, and stay warm, even if it's raining, windy and cold.

Gloves are worn no matter where you bike, usually biking gloves. Warmer gloves are needed for mountain areas. A sweatshirt or jogging jacket is comfortable, and is an extra layer.

If you camp, take **two pairs of shoes**—it's important to have a dry pair, in case you run into rain. If you're not camping, you can get by with one pair, and dry it out in your hotel.

Glasses of some kind are essential to keep dust, gravel, stones, insects, volcanic ash, and assorted other matter from getting into your eyes. If you wear prescription lenses, take a pair with plastic or hardened lenses. If you don't wear glasses, take sun glasses, clear lenses, or goggles that allow a good view.

I wear a reflective **security vest** over everything, of the kind used by road crews, whenever there is rain, fog, heavy traffic, darkness, or any other condition that would inhibit my being visible. The best reflective material is the type used by firemen on their raincoats, made of either glass fibers or glass prisms.

A **helmet** is recommended for security.

FOOD

Take along some tasty, lightweight, dry **food**, a lightweight alcohol **stove**, one sharp **knife**, and basic **utensils**. I'll have more to say about this topic later when I talk about life on the road.

CAMPING EQUIPMENT

Personally, I don't camp a lot in Latin America. I'm scared of spiders, snakes and giant ants. Also, hotels are usually reasonable, and there are few camping sites.

If you want to camp you need three items.

You have to bring a small, light, rain-resistant **tent**. North Face and Sierra Designs are good brands. It's essential to be dry.

You need a **mattress** or pad.

And a sleeping bag.

These three items, if light and compact, will easily fit on your bicycle.

Sometimes, in really cheap hotels, you ought to have a sleeping bag. One will also come in handy if you have the opportunity to stay in a private house.

OTHER EQUIPMENT

You need at least four **elastic straps** with hooks at each end. If you want to pack something extra onto your bicycle, if one of your pack bags breaks and you want to hold it together, if you have to tie your bike down on a boat or atop a bus, these straps are indispensable. When I travel on a bus, I remove my bicycle bags and attach them to the inside racks in such a way that nobody can grab my stuff and run. Straps will serve as clotheslines in hotels, to secure your hotel room door, to pack your bicycle onto a plane. You'll find straps in any hardware store.

I bring a small, sturdy **alarm clock** for when I have to get up early.

My **flashlight** is a scuba-diving model.

My **camera** is a Nikon with a small zoom lens. It resists vibrations—the screws on some cameras will work loose.

I use a Kryptonite **lock** with a hardened chain.

If you have any interests that require special equipment, make sure you take the sturdiest model.

3
PLANNING YOUR TRIP

For a good bicycle trip, as for a good meal, planning is essential.

- *Where are you going?*

- *Is it a place that holds some interest or fascination for you?*

- *What is the weather like at the time of year you will visit?*

There are other criteria to consider when you plan, but for me, these are the ones that will break or make a trip. You can be in worse-than-average physical condition, travel on lousy roads, wish you had better companions, and still have a worthwhile and enjoyable trip. But no matter how much you may be interested in Mayan ruins, you'll be miserable if you visit them in the rainy season. And if you go in the dry season and find Mayan ruins boring, you'll still be miserable.

Look at a map, and start eliminating countries. Are you afraid of war, unrest, civil turmoil? Strike out Chiapas in Mexico. You don't want flat landscapes? Eliminate the Caribbean coast of Mexico and Belize. On the other hand, include them as possibilities for a first trip if you don't want to be physically challenged, or if you'd like to bicycle-hop between extraordinary beaches. Guyana? Not enough roads to the interior. Afraid of thieves? Eliminate parts of Colombia, though there are fascinating possibilities (better for hiking, though). Colombians are Latin America's bicycle racing champions.

Once you've established the basics about your destination, start gathering useful information.

Buy a **guidebook** for the country you'll go to, and a map, if available, to check out the road system. Some titles and sources are mentioned at the end of this book. Consulates, tourist offices and the auto club can sometimes help.

Call or visit a **consulate** and see if you'll have any problem bringing in a bike. Are there any special regulations?

Learn some **Spanish** or **Portuguese**. I think a twenty-hour conversational course is sufficient for the needs of a cyclist, but a basic vocabulary will do. A Berlitz or similar phrase book will help, if you study in advance.

Go to a university library or a large public library. Try to find a **wind map** of the country you'll visit and use it to plan your best route. Often such a map will be included in an encyclopedia article. The encyclopedia will give you details on climate if you can't find a guide book with this information.

Get in shape for your tour. The best preparation is to take weekend trips. If you can last out a weekend, and even enjoy yourself a little, you shouldn't have any problems with the trips that I'll describe. There's not much difference between pedalling for a few days and going for a few weeks.

Make sure you're in good shape when you arrive for what you will be doing. I don't just mean for bicycling. If you're going to swim, then get in some practice laps.

Consider **how many people** will go together. The minimum—well, if you have an accident, it's nice to have another person around to help you out. The maximum—you can go with fifteen or sixteen if you want. But you're always waiting for someone or something before you can get started in the morning. Somebody has to fix a flat or has an upset stomach, and everyone else has to wait. Everyone needs air, but only one or two people have a pump. With five people, someone is always stopped for something. I think the maximum, really, is four. The more people you are, the more everyone will wait. And if at some point you have to catch a bus over part of your route, you won't be able to flag one down for your entire group.

How do you choose your companions? There are basically two types of bikers. If you like to bike for the sake of biking, you go with somebody with a similar approach. If you like to stop everywhere and poke around, you take along someone with a similar orientation. I think the best way to check out your companion is to take weekend trips. If you get along for a few days, chances are you can get along for a few weeks.

Not everyone in a group has to be in the same condition. Somebody in better shape can simply wait a few minutes for the others, rarely much longer. It's like jogging. If you arrive ten minutes earlier than your companions after an hour's run, you're in fantastically better shape than the others.

MORE DETAILS

It's important to have medical and hospital **insurance**, and insurance for your bike and other possessions. Many companies sell travellers policies that will cover most eventualities, but will not cover your bike. See if your homeowner's or renter's policy will cover your bike, and your liability if you run someone down.

Get any inoculations you need and make any other appropriate health preparations. I'll have more to say about this later.

Get your documents—**passport** and **visa**, or tourist card.

Think about how much **money** you will need, and how to carry it. Your guidebook should have recommendations for a specific country. I think it's better to bring a certain amount of cash and an ATM card and credit card than all travellers checks. You may find yourself in some remote towns where travellers checks are not trusted. Always bring American dollars. People look askance at other currencies. I usually figure on spending an average of $40 per day. For this amount I dine well and stay sometimes in excellent hotels. You can easily get by on much less, but it really is hard to spend a lot more. There are hardly any expenses with relation to the bicycle itself, and a bicycle tour does not go well with expensive high living. Nevertheless, you have to make a little provision for bad luck. A credit card will help if there are unforeseen expenses, either by charging them or getting a cash advance. Take some extra money as well.

4
GETTING THERE

Gather your baggage, tool kit, a beginning supply of food for the road, and other essentials.

Prepare your bicycle—acquire or change accessories as necessary for your trip. Have your wheels aligned at a bicycle store before you go. This costs just a few dollars.

PACKING YOUR BICYCLE

Most likely, you'll be taking your bicycle to your destination on an airplane. And in many cases, you will not be charged for taking it. Lucky you.

Whether it goes for free or not, you want your bike to arrive in one piece, so that your trip does not end before it starts.

I've seen recommendations in many books to pack your bike in a cardboard box. Well, it takes a very long time. And I have friends who have arrived to find their bikes damaged, even when they were well packed in boxes.

There are also some specialized carriers in which you can pack your bike. They can cost several hundred dollars, and they may be good. But I don't know what you would do with one of these things once you arrived in a country and started your tour.

Let me talk about a method that we've developed with experience. I think that if people who handle your bicycle can see it, they will take better care of it. If your bicycle is in a box, it's just a box. You can throw a box, drop a box, do with it what you want. But if your bicycle is visible, the handlers can see that it is obviously fragile.

So what I do is **wrap my bicycle in plastic**. Go to a hardware store and buy a large sheet of plastic for this purpose. It has to be at least 6 mil thick. A sufficient quantity will cost a few dollars.

First I take off the two pedals. Remember that the left pedal has a reverse thread. Put them in a plastic bag in your luggage. Leave your pump on the bicycle, but secure it with tape. Let some air out of each tire—low baggage-compartment pressure could conceivably cause them to balloon. Put your bike in the lowest gear so that the derailleur will be as far in as possible. Some bikes have a piece that protects the derailleur, which is a sensitive point. You can also stuff in some rags or foam.

Attach the front and rear wheels to the frame with elastic straps so that the wheels cannot turn. Loosen handlebars and turn them parallel to the frame, and put them in their lowest position. Also lower the saddle, but first nick the tube with your screwdriver to mark the correct riding height, otherwise you'll have to test your adjustments later. I also secure the handlebars to the frame with a strap.

Now, wrap your bike in plastic, being generous with your tape. Leave an opening where baggage handlers can grab the bicycle by the frame. This whole process takes about thirty minutes, maximum.

Once your bike is ready, consider your luggage. If you have accessible zippers on your bike bags, ask the airline for a luggage box in which to stow them. Items have been pilfered from my bags a couple of times. Those zipper compartments do not lock. But a box will delay and probably deter a thief. A large plastic bag could also do. You're allowed, generally, two pieces of luggage. If one is your bicycle, the other is your bicycle bags. If there's no box or plastic bag available, tape them together to make one piece. Of course, remove all valuables. Once, I forgot to remove a large amount of cash from the compartment of one of my bags before checking it. But I was lucky. It was the other compartment that was opened.

ROUTING

When possible, I try to get myself and my bicycle to my destination on a single airline. That way, if there's any damage to my bicycle, there won't be any question of one airline pointing an accusing finger at another.   Only one can be responsible.

It's also a good idea to attach a sticker to your bicycle with your name and address, in case your bike goes astray in transit.

GOING

Plan your transport to the airport. If you call a taxi in the morning, you may find that the driver doesn't want to take your bicycle. Plan to ride out, or verify that the public bus or a particular taxi company will take your bike. Get a good night's sleep before you start, and go slow on the in-flight booze. Air travel is hard enough on the system.

ARRIVING

In most airports, the first thing you do after you get off the plane is pick up your luggage. I recommend that once you have your bike, you get to work right away and assemble it, in the baggage area. This is usually well-lighted, away from crowds, questions, interruptions, prying hands, and curious eyes. If something is broken, you will see it right off, and be able to file a claim with the airline.

When you unpack your bike, cut the tape from the plastic, and tie the plastic to your bike rack with one of your elastic straps. You can use it for the return trip, but it will probably be finished for any further use, and will have grease on it anyway.

Be especially careful when attaching your pedals. It's too easy to strip the threads. Be gentle and align well. My great fear is that someday I will forget my pedals.

There is always a bathroom in the customs area. After you assemble your bike, use the bathroom to change into your biking clothes, like Superman going into his phone booth.

When you come out, put your luggage on your bike instead of lugging it on your back—an advantage in getting to and through the customs inspection. Then proceed into the world outside, and good luck.

5
ON THE ROAD

In this section I'll cover two very important topics: your health and your food. Then I'll go over daily routines, practices, obstacles, and problems, and try to give you assorted tips.

STAYING HEALTHY ON THE ROAD

Let me turn the podium over to Natalie Rivest, M.D. Natalie has been my companion on a number of bicycle trips, and consulted specialists in the problems of travellers to prepare this talk.

Natalie . . .

Volume and weight are, of course, of the essence when you are bicycle touring. You should bring only what is necessary in the way of first-aid and health protection. Just as important, learn to avoid problems, or recognize and treat them early.

You can divide your emergency kit into

(1) what you'll need in case of accident;

(2) medication for conditions in the country you're travelling in, and for bicycling ailments, such as sunburn; and

(3) medication that you regularly take, if any.

If you have a collision or fall, you'll want to clean your wound immediately. You'll use clean drinking **water** and

soap, both of which you carry anyway; **gauze** or clean cloth to dress the wound; and **adhesive tape** to close gaping wounds, until you can get proper medical attention. **Band-aids** are useful to cover smaller wounds and blisters. These last items are all lightweight, and can be replenished easily at any pharmacy while you travel.

Be prepared for the local climate. Sunburn can be a problem almost anywhere. Take a **sunscreen cream** containing PABA. I take one cream with an 8 rating and one with a 15 rating. Apply it to all exposed areas. Don't forget the upper surface of your hands, which spend the day taking the sun on the handlebars. This area takes a 15 for sure, as does your nose, which suffers not only direct sun, but the reflection from your glasses as well. Less exposed areas take an 8. As you tan, you can lessen the sun rating of the cream you apply, or eliminate it from certain body areas altogether. If you burn anyway, you'll need a cream with zinc oxide—the same stuff used for diaper rash. This ointment will also soothe irritated skin on your seat and between your thighs, and can be applied to your lips for chapping.

Take **insect repellent** if insects are likely to be a problem. The best active ingredient is methyl toluamide. One brand name is Muskol, another is Cutter.

Inquire beforehand about **endemic diseases** in the countries you're going to. Your local public health department can inform you on the risks and inoculate you against yellow fever, typhoid, and other diseases. Your public health clinic or personal physician can prescribe tablets to protect you against malaria.

Take twice the quantity of **personal medicines** that you think you'll need. The extra weight is insignificant, and you might not easily find the brand name you're familiar with. Think about your personal susceptibilities. If you dislocated your shoulder five years ago, take along a muscle relaxant in case it acts up or dislocates again. If you have ever had asthmatic or allergic attacks or anaphylactic reactions, bring appropriate bronchodilator, pills, or whatever it is that gives you relief.

If there is any chance of a new sexual relationship, be prepared with **condoms**.

In summary, your medical kit should include:

- Halazone or bleach for drinking water

- sunscreen cream

- aspirin or another analgesic

- sterile pads

- bandages

- your personal medicines; and, possibly,

- malaria tablets, insect repellent, zinc oxide and condoms.

I don't want to be alarmist, but you should be generally aware of the kinds of diseases you can find in tropical countries. In some areas, you can catch schistosomiasis, simply by swimming in fresh water inhabited by certain snails. If you can't find information where you live (at bookstores or in libraries), write to the addresses given in the More Information section of this book.

For snake bite, the best vaccines, specific to the venom of local species, will be found in each country. Watch where you step, and avoid the problem.

THE RIGHT ACCESSORIES

Bicycle gloves are essential to cushion your hands and protect them in a spill. Contact lenses are hard on some people when it's warm and sunny. If you have this problem, wear prescription sunglasses instead. And, as Jean-Pierre said, wear some sort of glasses all the time even if you don't use corrective lenses, in order to protect yourself from flying gravel, dust, etc. Photosensitive lenses that darken in proportion to the intensity of sunlight are very practical.

PREVENTING PROBLEMS—AND DEALING WITH THEM

Heat prostration and dehydration are best treated by prevention—wearing a **hat** and drinking enough water. Eat potato chips when you stop at a country store—they have salt, which you need. If the heat gets to you, you'll have to get into the shade, and relax. A sure sign of dehydration is infrequent urination.

For traveller's **diarrhea** from unfamiliar foods, drink plenty of liquids to replace lost body fluids—fruit juice with added sugar and a generous dash of salt is ideal. Stick to rice and plain pasta until you feel better. For painful diarrhea, with more than a dozen bowel movements a day, see a doctor.

It's good to get off your bicycle every now and then and stretch your arms and legs. If you stay in the same position for hours, you're sure to get cramps. You can also get cramps from lack of sufficient salt.

Thank you, Dr. Rivest.

FOOD AND DRINK ON THE ROAD

In general—and there are exceptions to this, but you better not count on them—sanitary conditions in Latin America are suspect. You can get sick enough to ruin your trip by consuming the food and water in some local eateries. But not to worry, at least, not too much. I am living proof that it is possible to survive and even prosper on the local food resources.

First of all, take a few precautions, and change some of your habits.

- Do not eat green salads anywhere.

- Do not eat in doubtful-looking places.

- Do not drink unpasteurized milk, in fact, avoid milk products even if they claim to be pasteurized. They may not be, and they spoil quickly in the tropics anyway.

- Make sure everything is well cooked.

- If you have a choice of restaurants, go to one with a lot of clients who look happy. Look at the food on the plates. Follow the advice of a good guidebook, if you have one. It's fun to make food discoveries on your own, but sometimes those discoveries can be unpleasant.

- Drink bottled liquids only. Outside of most major cities, and even in some of them, water is polluted. Everyone knows this except the unsuspecting traveller. Fortunately, at least for you, bottled soft drinks are available almost everywhere in Latin America. You don't have to search out a supermarket. Even in the smallest hamlets where electricity, running water and a gasoline pump are lacking, every little corner store and stand has a supply of warm Coca-Cola (or Inca Cola, as the case may be). As a side benefit, sodas give you an energy lift with their high sugar content. If you get tired of that sticky feeling on your teeth, you can buy plain soda water, mineral water, purified water in sealed plastic containers, or, usually, small cans of juices. When you can't buy soft drinks, boil your water for fifteen minutes. Or treat it with Halazone, or, less conveniently, a couple of drops of laundry bleach per liter. Make sure you let it stand a half-hour. Also treat any water you use to reconstitute dry foods.

YOUR MENU

My style of bicycle travel is not a survival expedition. I prefer to eat in restaurants and roadside diners. But I always carry some food that I can prepare easily, in case the local cuisine looks unhealthy, or merely unsavory. There are lots of goodies to choose from. Packaged dry soups are the basis for many a meal on the road. Local market vegetables and rice can be tossed in the pot for variety and substance. A modest amount of herbs and spices will make your repast more interesting. Other lightweight items are herbal teas, freeze-dried foods sold in camping stores, and even instant baby food for real emergencies (e.g., Heinz turkey and vegetables). Health food stores are good sources of supply for instant hummous, vegetarian burgers, and dry tofu. Start with a modest stock, and replenish with local products on the road. Packaged dry soups, rice, teas, flavorings and similar products are available to a greater or lesser extent wherever you go. Make sure you select foods that you won't turn up your nose at.

For cooking, I take along an **alcohol stove**. Stoves are available that run on white gasoline, kerosene or bottled gas, but you can't count on finding fuel. On the other hand, alcohol—usually *alcohol de caña*, made from sugar cane but also isopropyl rubbing alcohol—is available everywhere, in liquor stores, village general stores, and pharmacies. I use a Triga alcohol stove, made in Sweden. This particular kind is available in camping stores throughout the United States and Canada. It has a small burner, and comes with a compact, nesting set of **pots**—very handy. The only problem I've had with it is that it blows out easily in any wind. You'll have to use it in a sheltered place. Note that isopropyl alcohol should have a concentration of at least 70 percent to be used as a fuel.

For implements, bring a small, sharp **knife**. One will do for your group. Keep it sheathed when not in use. One **tablespoon** per person is needed. I have never found forks indispensable, but you might. Take one plastic **bowl** per person, if your stove doesn't come with plates. Also one plastic **cup**.

Do I have to tell you that eating well and staying in good health are necessary parts of bicycle touring? Eat a good dinner and a good breakfast. You may want to go light on lunch when you're in the saddle, but make sure you get enough liquid. If you have the slightest doubt about the local eateries, never hesitate to take the time to cook for yourself. If you get sick, you'll either be unable to continue your trip, or do so only with great difficulty. Sure, there are dread tropical diseases, but the easiest way to get sick is from bad food or water.

DAILY ROUTINES

Here are some suggested routines and assorted tips to make your trip easier, safer, and more enjoyable.

Each morning, before you leave, check your bike. Touch the spokes, the tires, look around at the brake cables, see if anything is loose or falling off. A spoke that is about to break has a characteristic sound. You can prevent accidents and loss of equipment this way, or at least put the odds on your side. See that screws are tight. And if you hear a rattle while riding, stop and see what it is about, and tighten up whatever is loose.

Figure out a good day's journey before you set out. Take local conditions into account. Is it very hot? Is the terrain mountainous and will you be going uphill? In either case, your speed may be reduced. Are you going on a paved or gravel road? Your speed could be halved on the latter. Are there places to stop for the night? It's better to call a halt before you end up in the middle of nowhere after dark.

Usually, it's better to ride in the morning. You're fresh, there's less wind, and you can take it easy and visit places in the afternoon. If you're up at 7:30, you can be on the road at 9, and stop at 2:30 or 3 in the afternoon.

Don't try to bike each day. Stop after five days or so, and take a good rest. Sit around the pool, forget about the road.

If you are tired, if your knees hurt, stop. If you go on pushing yourself over a period of weeks or months, the damage will accumulate each day. It's better to cover a smaller distance for the day.

If you are more than one, you have to maintain contact. If one of you takes a wrong turn, everyone loses at least

41

double the time he's travelled, between going and returning. Attempting to find lost companions could turn a good day into a bad day. Always maintain eye contact.

Use signals to communicate. I have only a few that are important. When there is a hole or obstacle, I point down to it to indicate it to those behind me. If you have to stop, you put your arm down with your hand open. To signal a right turn, put your left hand up, and to signal a left turn, extend your left hand straight out. Sand on a paved road is as dangerous as ice for a car. When one of us notices it, he waves his arm back and forth. You can make up your own signs, but insist that your companions use them. It's a matter of security.

PRACTICE SAFE CYCLING

It's a good idea to test your brakes before you start a long descent. When you go down a hill for more than two or three minutes—down a volcano, or from an Andean pass, say—stop every five minutes. Touch the rim of your wheel. If it's hot, take a break and let it cool off. If you let your tire continue to heat up, it can melt, or explode. Remember, with the weight of your luggage, your brakes will have more work to do. One trick is to brake at the front for a few minutes, then the back, allowing some of the heat to dissipate alternately as you go along.

Accelerate just before changing gears, then release the gear lever while still pedalling. The chain will move to its new position more easily. Change gears as soon as you encounter extra resistance.

With luggage over your front wheel, you have to make slower, smoother turns than you would when not carrying luggage. Also, remember that you're wider with your bags sticking out.

When it is rainy or foggy, be visible, even if there is no traffic. Use a reflective safety vest, if you can get one.

Dirt roads are especially skiddy when wet.

On gravel, watch out for snakes.

Some cyclists take dog repellent. But it's only in North America, that you find spoiled, dangerous dogs. In Latin America, where dogs are ill-treated and afraid of humans, I have never seen a dangerous dog. My own trick, when a dog approaches with its mouth open, is to grab my pump and wave it as if I am going to brain the dog. In 95 percent of the cases, the dog turns tail. The other five percent haven't occurred yet. Another way is to throw a rock, or pretend you're throwing a rock.

As for cattle, they generally don't chase after you.

When there is wind, it helps to bike in close formation to cut the wind's force, especially if you have heavy luggage.

TIPS FOR HAPPIER TRAVEL

When you ask directions, always inquire for the next village on the map and no further. Country people in Latin America have often not been farther than the next town. Asking them for the way to a large city might be like asking the way to Mars. And ask twice (of different people, of course).

Never ride at night unless absolutely necessary
.

If you go to buy something in a store, make sure somebody in the group watches your bike. The chances of somebody taking your bike with all your equipment and baggage is quite small—they probably won't be able to ride it—but you never know. If you find yourself alone and leave your bike for a moment, leave it in high gear. Nobody can then ride off without the telltale click-clack of changing gears.

Never, under any circumstances, leave your bicycle on the street at night. Ask permission to take your bike into your hotel room. If this is not permitted, try to store it in a locked garage or luggage room. Lock your bike any time it's unattended. It helps to tip a guard as well. Your bike is worth a year's salary in some countries. I use just a short hardened chain and a Kryptonite lock. Lock two bikes together as well as to a pipe or some other stationary object. But don't over-worry. You don't have the specialized bicycle thieves that we have in North American cities.

When you can, choose a quiet hotel or a room away from the street. You want a good night's sleep. It's easy to find and look for hotels, so make sure you choose well.

If you want to take a bus, be prepared to help convince a possibly reluctant driver to take you and your bike. Have the front wheel off, and put your bicycle into the baggage compartment or on top yourself if you have to.

On the bus or train, travel with your bicycle. Don't let it be put on another train or bus.

If salt water splashes on your bicycle (say, on a ferry), rinse it off at the first opportunity in order to prevent rusting.

Ask for permission to camp. Formal campgrounds are in short supply in Latin America. There are many places to pitch your tent in the countryside, but just make sure the people about know what you're up to.

Convenient small sizes of detergent are generally available. Buy these instead of relying on hand soap.

If I'm with a female companion, I let her carry the money, since everyone thinks it's the man who has it. She puts all valuables—money, passport and return tickets—in a plastic bag, and in a security belt when we hit a town.

Sleep with your camera and money under your pillow, if you're worried.

6
DOMINICAN REPUBLIC

The Dominican Republic is not too far away from North America, and its tourist facilities are expanding rapidly. One of the attractions of going now is to be there before the boom. The north coast is replete with white, sandy beaches, and there are good if not outstanding locales for scuba diving. Warm weather is guaranteed. There are even some historical attractions: Santo Domingo, the capital, is the oldest European city in the New World, the point from which Spain conquered America.

Other countries have roughly similar attractions. But I had been to Haiti, and was curious about the other part of the island of Hispaniola, which is the second largest in the Caribbean. Besides, it had been a cold winter, I had a week off in April, and I heard of a good charter fare. So I read up on the country, and off I flew, with friend and our bikes.

Despite the justified image of an island planted in sugar cane, there is some variety to the Dominican Republic. The Cordillera Central, a range running down the western side of the country, tops off at Duarte Peak, the highest point in the Caribbean at over 3000 meters (10,000 feet). There are lesser

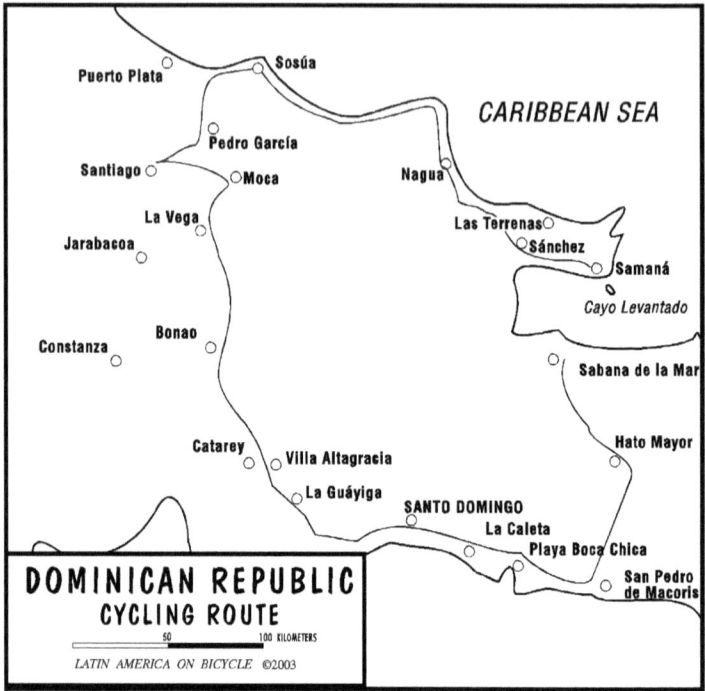

DOMINICAN REPUBLIC
CYCLING ROUTE
50   100 KILOMETERS
LATIN AMERICA ON BICYCLE ©2003

mountains backdropping the beaches of the north coast. Most of the landscape consists of rolling hills and valleys.

The Dominican Republic shares the island of Hispaniola with Haiti, but aside from proximity and ecosystems, the two nations have neither language nor level of living in common. The Dominican Republic is poor, but is wealthy compared to Haiti. Most people in the Dominican Republic look like Michael Jackson, slim, brown, curly-haired mulattos. There are pockets of blacks of Haitian heritage, modern-day slaves who are consigned to the lowest jobs cutting sugar cane and doing menial labor in the cities.

For the bicyclist, there are roads everywhere. They're not in excellent shape, but for the slow pace appropriate to the climate, most are more than adequate. Roads near Santo

Domingo—the capital—along the south central coast, and to Santiago and the north coast are the most heavily trafficked. The Dominican Republic is not a huge country—just slightly larger than Denmark.

Even with only a week's stay, distances are such that you'll get the feeling of having really seen what this country is about, yet you won't be going around in circles. Nor will you get lost—even the worst roads are well posted with concrete signs marking the distance from the next town.

From May through November it rains for a few hours almost every day, with considerable letup in July. November to April are the dry months, with December and January probably the best time for a visit—not sweltering, but practically guaranteed rainless. We went in April, and I never biked so much—I must have made a twelve-day trip in seven days. If you're not constrained by charter flight schedules, as I was, a better plan is to allow three weeks to travel through both Haiti and the Dominican Republic.

Neither I nor my companion, who was on her first Latin-American bike trip and was in better shape than me, found the rolling terrain overly challenging. The countryside is well populated, there are little stores and eateries all over for re-stocking and quenching your thirst. We ate everywhere with the usual precautions—no unpeeled fruits, bottled beverages—and our tummies enjoyed the trip. It would be a good idea to bring a small stove, though in fact we never cooked for ourselves. Nor did wind, thieves or other villains and gremlins trouble us.

But the sun is strong and must always be kept in mind. I burned through my thin t-shirt. Malaria preventative tablets are recommended.

Hotels in the interior of the island can be basic, but good accommodations are available in the mushrooming tourist centers on the north coast. As it was near Easter, we weren't always able to stay at the hotel of our choice. Hotel prices are slightly lower than in North America.

The official tourist map of the Dominican Republic is essential for the cyclist. Though not greatly detailed, it indicates the best roads and major points of interest, and is available at Dominican tourist offices in the United States and Canada. More detailed black-and-white maps, on a scale of 1:672,000, are available at bookstores and corner stores in the country, and are useful for figuring out exactly where you are. Dominican consulates and tourist offices are under instructions to do everything they can to promote tourism, and are quite helpful.

We rode on 18-speed touring bikes. Only a few of the roads we took were gravel-surfaced and would have been more suitable to mountain bikes. If you include Haiti in your trip, then by all means take a mountain bike.

Our clothing was lighter for this trip than it usually is. No heavy sweater is needed, unless you tackle the road up to Constanza in the Cordillera Central. But take a raincoat just in case—some parts of the country are subject to occasional downpours even in the dry season.

Bicycle stores and parts will not be easily found in the countryside, but if you have a major breakdown, you're never more than a few hours by bus from Santo Domingo or Santiago, where you should be able to get parts and service. Buses run practically everywhere from the capital. Microbuses, which cram more than a dozen people aboard, will somehow find a place for your bicycle among the baskets and cardboard boxes in the luggage rack. Fares are low. Larger (and more comfortable) intercity buses will generally not take you aboard at mid-route.

DAY ONE

We arrived at 3 a.m. at Las Américas airport after a four-hour charter flight from Montreal. Our fellow passengers, no sober business travellers, took advantage of the free champagne during the whole flight. So there was a lot of action on the plane, and no sleep. We passed through customs, took our bikes from their cardboard boxes, assembled them to the stares of the throngs, and headed out, the night lit up by the fires of squatters living among the trees beside the road.

The sun was rising as we neared La Caleta on the expressway to the capital, traffic was heavy, reflective safety vests were necessary . . . and we didn't have any. Jitney taxis cruised the road, stopping and starting constantly, picking up and discharging passengers. With as many as ten people shoehorned into rear seats, doors flopped out, unable to close, threatening to whack any pedestrian or cyclist in their way. The highway was a desolate town in itself, lined with stands and ambulant vendors selling food, newspapers and anything merchantable. The frenzy intensified as we approached Santo Domingo. The edges of the roads merged into bidonvilles, there were no real suburbs or developed towns or church spires popping out along the road.

By 8 a.m. we had covered the 30 kilometers to the edge of the capital. The expressway turned into Avenida de las Américas, and rush-hour traffic was dense. We crossed the Ozama River, a true río de mierda, lined with shacks built of trash.

It was breakfast time when we arrived, so we temporarily left the traffic and noise and commerce on one of the main streets of a Latin American capital, through a space and time warp, into the North American world of the as-yet-uncompleted Hotel Lina, where quiet, air-conditioning and Muzak reigned.

After breakfast, we took a breath of cool air, and re-entered the city. Westward we cycled, back toward the city limits. We knew we'd be in the capital at the end of our trip, and nothing we saw made us want to delay now. Mostly, we crossed poor neighborhoods, but also some substantial residential areas. We passed several military bases.

We left town by the Autopista Duarte, a flat, heavily trafficked two-lane highway, heading toward Santiago, the country's second city. We shouldn't have taken this road on bicycle. Traffic was so dense that cars continually crowded us off the right shoulder, demanding passage.

At the edge of the city, soldiers with fixed bayonets manned a toll booth. They demanded payment. We paid. In the Dominican Republic, we didn't have the impression of social unrest, or of an oppressive government. But the military lurks. The soldier gave us no receipt.

What I don't understand about that highway is that there were no main intersecting roads, and yet, after about fifteen kilometers, traffic began to thin out. The trucks just disappeared.

Beyond Santo Domingo we entered hilly country, dry at this time of year. For ten kilometers the road is lined with shanty towns of people trying to survive at the most basic level. But soon we were in the countryside, and the slums gave out. We pulled over from time to time at bus stops to rest and have a drink and receive the not unfriendly stares of the waiting Michael Jacksons.

Near La Guáyiga, we saw a circle of people milling about,. a commotion at the center. We stopped, approached on foot, and were let into a small ring to see a cock fight in progress— no charge for tourists. Signs advised spectators to get their bets in before the start of the match. We watched for more than an hour, in a cloud of plumes. The winning cock was taken out to a small infirmary for patching up. People tried to explain the action to us, and egged us on to make bets.

From La Guáyiga, we went on, still in heavy traffic, past names on the map that hardly existed on the ground, and reached Villa Altagracia, about 60 kilometers from Santo Domingo, by 2 p.m. There were no particular attractions, just luxuriant green growth along the dusty streets. But it was warm, and with our sleepless night and early start, we were quite tired. The Hotel Bronx beckoned to us, and, I would guess from appearances, to couples who could not shack up in classier surroundings.

A good half of the village gathered around to see us, innocent real tourists, heading for these digs. The place was so basic that it was clean—there was nothing to get dirty, just plywood cubicles, and cots with a couple of sheets. No showers, no car-rental agency. I have a photo of my companion standing in front of the hotel, with throngs of locals, and I suppose that it could be mistaken for some part of the borough of the Bronx in midsummer. We stayed an hour, took a bath by scooping water from a barrel, talked to each other in conversational tones between our separate rooms, and watched the salamanders going up and down the plywood. Fans were brought, it was all like a dream for me, the fans droning at the mosquitoes, and I half dozing, waking and not remembering where or why I was, hearing moos and voices calling in the choppy language, and cocks crowing.

When the sun went down we tried the village for food. We had roast something, and retreated to our cots. We heard the village sounds no longer, it was Sunday night and the Hotel Bronx was in full frenzy. We slept anyway.

DAY TWO

We were up at 5 a.m. We took a side road from the main highway to Catarey, pleased at the break from heavy traffic, but there was no way to continue, so we retraced our route. Eateries dotted the highway, we stopped whenever we felt like drinking something, which was often, and had our pick of good food. The landscape was agricultural all the way, rolling, with no big peaks at the horizon, just more of the same.

Forty kilometers past Villa Altagracia we took another side road, into Bonao. It looked from the map to be a major town, we thought we'd find something interesting. But it was just a small, quiet place. We continued, past the junction for the road to Constanza, high in the Cordillera Central. With more time we would have gone that way—it's supposed to be a slice of Swiss scenery. We also should have stopped at the ruins of Vega Vieja, founded by Christopher Columbus, and destroyed in 1564. But we were anxious to get to the sea and the beach. We branched from the main highway toward Moca, making a dog leg in order to escape the heavy traffic to Santiago. This part of the island was greener, but still dry.

We were in Moca by 4 p.m., a journey too long already for this hot climate. What we should have done was to take the left fork at La Vega, toward Jarabacoa. The South American Handbook mentions a good hotel, the Montaña, along the way. We could have cycled up to Constanza and back down the next day, or simply continued northward. But we didn't stop in Moca, either. We considered heading up a mountain to an important religious sanctuary, and views. But we were too hot. Instead, we drank sodas at a store, and found ourselves besieged by sounds from a building across the street, harsh, cawing cries, and hands stretched out. It was a jail. In our shorts we might have looked as strange as their gesticulating hands and cries seemed to us. We were uncomfortable, but we, at least, could move on, and we did, as the arghs followed us.

The road we took was being constructed or improved— they may be working on it still. We crossed wooden bridges, slowed down, stopped, started.

There isn't much to see in this area, it is all flat country, dusty, with an occasional shantytown. The land was cleared long ago, but nothing much grows there now. I think that we ourselves were the main attraction wherever we went. And the local bikes were also curious for us. One had no tires, no pedals, only two bars where the pedals should have been, and a pump. The rider just coasted along.

We were in Santiago by 6 p.m., at sunset, and pooped. We pulled up to the Hotel Camino Real, and I left my companion outside while I went in to ask the price. They told me it was $25 double, and I went back outside and sat down, too exhausted to make any move toward checking in. It must have looked from the inside as if the price was too high for us, for a guy came out and offered us the room for $18. We looked at each other, cried "sí!," but still took another ten minutes before getting up and moving in. The hotel had seven or eight stories, and a restaurant on top where we ate, too tired to appreciate the view. The food was chicken and steaks, not native-style, not elegant either—the sanitary "international" cuisine that Latin American hotels think their guests desire.

Later, from the room, my friend, wanting to practice her Spanish, ordered three lemonades. Or thought so, as she repeated her order to the room service operator, who for some reason questioned her request. Knock, knock, knock, we opened the door, and there was the boy with thirteen lemonades. Trece, not tres. She paid, we were thirsty anyway.

DAY THREE

Breakfast was good, we were able at least to appreciate the view in the morning. Red tile roofs predominate in Santiago, giving a colonial air to the city. Several bridges span the Jaragua River, the stuccoed building façades could be somewhere in South America, far from any sea. Traffic was dense. In the distance, cultivated fields spread out into the hills, fog lingered here and there. The massive monument to the heroes of the restoration, dedicated to the dictator Trujillo, was visible.

Before leaving, we went to look for water, for we were going to cross the Cordillera Septentrional, the northern coastal mountain ridge. We leaned our bikes against a wall, I entered a store, and bought the purified water, which comes in a squarish plastic bottle, usually covered with dust. When I came out, I found somebody asking my friend for money. She was giving him a lot of money, I didn't understand why, if not just to get rid of him. But then I saw that he had a disease, it looked like leprosy. His skin was coming off, he was missing a hand, he was approaching her and feinting as if to touch her if she didn't give him money. It worked.

We headed north, taking a side road from Palo Quemado to avoid heavy traffic. We could have continued back on the main highway west and then northeast to Puerto Plata, on the north coast, but we wanted to tour a little in the mountains. So, after a quick, flat run of about 25 kilometers to Pedro García, we turned onto the mountain road to Tubagua. This is actually a shorter road to the sea, but it climbs steadily. We ascended a thousand meters, past banana plants and other lush foliage, and looked down on the vast Santiago valley cultivated as far as we could see. The asphalt gradually thinned and finally ended by the time we reached the summit, ten kilometers past the junction at Pedro García. It looked like we were heading to a dead end, but every once in a while a microbus came up, chugged alongside us, and finally picked up enough speed to move ahead, and didn't come back our way. We stopped at mountain villages for sodas, the inhabitants came out of their poor houses and crowded around to see the cyclists.

Beyond the summit, where two pillars marked the provincial boundary, the road was gravel, and poorly kept. Negotiating it on a touring bike was difficult. The road was flat, then went down gradually, then went up, then down again. For five kilometers we followed the crest of a ridge, and could look down to either side. We came to Tubagua, and entered another time. A bridge crossed a river, near it were colonial houses of a type I had seen only in films, thick-walled, tile-roofed, stucco peeling off. They belonged to a coffee plantation. We pedalled upward again, at 2 p.m. at the height of the day's heat, past houses built of bamboo and banana leaves that a gust of wind could have carried off. At the first intersection, at about 3 p.m., 30 kilometers out of Pedro García, we turned right to reach the paved coastal road. But first we came across a shop, where, if you come this way, I recommend that you stop, even if you do not need anything. It gave us the feeling of having travelled back fifty years, to a small-town general store. People walked in and left with huge sacks of rice on their backs. Others bought nails. People sat around and shot the breeze over Cokes. Dust sat on the counter. We filled up on Cokes ourselves.

Back on pavement, with some traffic, we pedalled the 15 kilometers to Sosúa in 45 minutes, the wind at our backs, through plantations of sugar cane twice as high as a man, and higher. We arrived at about 4:30 p.m.

We headed for the beach, and visited most of the hotels. They were crowded, it was the beginning of the Holy Week holiday season. Loudspeakers blasted the music of Michael Jackson to accompany the bathing and sunning Michael Jacksons. It was enough Michael Jackson for me. There is supposed to be a Jewish community in the area, dairy farmers become hotel owners, who arrived as refugees from Hitler. We stayed in the clean Hotel Sosúa where all rooms face a pool, for about $14 double with poolside breakfast. We jumped in the pool, and relaxed.

DAY FOUR

We stayed two nights in Sosúa. There is said to be good snorkeling offshore—we didn't do any—but I can report that there are good restaurants. And there will be more of them by the time you cycle in, such is the pace of building and development. We moved to Nino's Hotel, where friends were staying. The rate was about $40 for a cabin, for as many people as could crowd in, and this with functioning hot water and air conditioning. Barring blackouts, that is. Following a small electrical storm, we lost the air conditioning for a whole sweaty night.

We cycled out to some of the deserted, palm-fringed beaches along the coast road to the east. There are other deserted beaches west of Puerto Plata, the other end of this Dominican Riviera. They look deserted, anyway. No matter where you go, a nature boy appears from behind a palm, machete in hand. You think that he is going to rob you, you get ready to grab your towel and run for your bicycle to outrace him. But no, he is offering his services, to climb up a palm and knock down a coconut and eviscerate it and open up the inner, juicy kernel, all for 25 cents.

DAY FIVE

We left Sosúa in the morning, headed toward Samaná, 185 kilometers away, at the eastern end of the north coast. This would be a good day's outing at home, but we thought it would be otherwise in tropical heat and sun on roads not always well maintained, even if mostly flat. So we were up at sunrise and flagged down the first microbus that came along. We rode about half the way to our destination, then got on our bicycles again.

We had a strange experience at Nagua. We were caught with our bicycles in a funeral procession, people on foot, and trucks full of people inching along. I don't know who had died, but it was quite an event. Some people carried flowers, people on trucks were dancing. Nagua as a town was just a town.

We were following the coast, separated from the water only by coconut palms and sand. Sometimes, we saw people drying cocoa beans on the asphalt. We stopped to taste the beans, and chat with the workers. The road turned inland, and we reached the strange village of Sánchez around 12:30 p.m. Sánchez is the end-point of a derelict plantation railroad, an insular and abandoned-looking place. The railroad station, its tin roof, the tracks, the stranded rail cars are all rusting away among weeds. And the weeds grow to huge heights quickly in the tropics. We bought food at a supermarket, saw jeeps coming in and leaving with supplies for the plantations, the town was surviving as an entrepot even without the railway.

A dirt road branches northeast from Sánchez up to a height of 350 meters, then descends again to the coast at Las Terrenas. To the east of Las Terrenas are some of the best undeveloped beaches of the Dominican Republic, all reached by this poor road. A film about Christopher Columbus was being shot along this stretch of coast, but we didn't go that way on our touring bikes. Instead, we took the paved road directly to the east.

We had had an easy ride, the signs indicated that we were five kilometers from Samaná, we thought we would end our day on the road in a matter of minutes. But in the final stretch we had to climb a large hill, at least 150 meters high—good for views at least—before descending into Samaná, a pleasant city. When we got to the main square, people approached and asked if we wanted to rent a room. But we saw the large Hotel Cayacoa on a little Sugar Loaf above town, and headed toward it. We found that they expected groups the next day, but they could give us a room for the night. Facilities were excellent at this little paradise—pool, private beach reached by a stairway down the cliff, windsurfers for rent. At night, overtired as usual, we enjoyed a jazz show and buffet.

DAY SIX

We took a trip to Cayo Levantado, an offshore island, on a boat that had about triple the number of passengers that it should have carried. The motor broke down, the crowd aboard was terrified, until we were taken in tow by a boat that had about five times the number of people it should have carried. After an hour and a half we reached the island, set amid crystalline waters. Vendors sold food, and boys played music on contraptions made of scrap wood and metal, screwed, hammered and wired together. They looked strange, old-fashioned, like no instruments I knew. A piece of wood trilled against a metal sheet punctured by nails—a sort of grater. A square wooden box had an arched opening, standing strips of wood inside were plunked, they vibrated with a surprisingly pleasing sound. A drum looked to have been made from a garbage can. The musicians' fee was negotiable—about 25 cents for most songs.

When we returned to Samaná we arranged to move into a private home. We were given one room, a whole family had rented another room, and, as far as we could see, stayed put in it. We, in turn, had our own guests, an extended family of cockroaches, who watched us all night.

DAY SEVEN

We took a boat across the Bay of Samaná, getting up early to make sure of getting a place. We didn't think that the number of people on the wharf could fit on the boat for the 20-kilometer crossing to Sabana de La Mar. But they did. The waves hit the boat broadside from the east, the boat was rolling all the time, I saw the sea, then the sky then the sea then the sky. If you're prone to seasickness, a trip like this will finish you off. I think that on a windy day the crossing must be impossible. Our bikes went inside along with everyone else's baggage. I secured them with an elastic strap, having expected some rolling, though not in fact what we experienced. Everyone fell asleep in the end.

It took about an hour and a half to cross to Sabana de la Mar, where there was no dock. We were offloaded into small boats for the trip ashore, and on the way the clouds burst. There were sharks around, our frightened fellow passengers cried, and we could have turned over at any moment. It was action and tension for five minutes. But we arrived intact.

We left Sabana de la Mar and its houses built on piles, and cycled southeast across hills to Hato Mayor, then southward over flat country. The pavement was in good shape, and it went quite well on bicycle. We took about five hours to get to San Pedro de Macoris, 85 kilometers away on the south coast. Cacao is grown in the northern part of this area, on plantations worked by Haitians.

There was more traffic, we found, on the road along the sea. So seven kilometers out of San Pedro de Macoris, we took a microbus for Playa Boca Chica, where we planned to stop for our last swim.

Well, let me say now that nobody should ever, ever go to Playa Boca Chica. It was the height of the Easter vacation season, and all of Santo Domingo had turned out. The green water had become brown. Derelict hotels were full of people squatting and dancing and reveling. I had never seen a place as unpleasant and spoiled as that one, and it wasn't the foreigners who had done it. There must have been 30,000 or 40,000, maybe even 50,000 on a small beach. We stopped there because I had seen some brochures at home for Playa Boca Chica. So much for promotional material. It was impossible, with all those people, to have any fun, there was tension in the air. With more time, we might have gone back east, past San Pedro de Macoris to La Romana, where there are pleasant beaches, some reached only by boat. But our plane was to leave the next morning at 6 a.m.

Our plans botched, we had no choice but to go on into Santo Domingo. And there we stayed at a very, very nice hotel in the old city, the Hostal Nicolás de Ovando, a restored sixteenth-century mansion named for a colonial governor. Food was excellent, the atmosphere was romantic, from the pool we had a view onto the Ozama River, which at this end was not lined with shanties. The fortress was closed, but we tipped a guard to let us in to see the massive stone structures, created at what was one of the ends of the world at the time. It was worth coming back to see the historic city.

While strolling through the old town, we saw a lot of men with green hats, and elegant uniforms, looking like an elite squad. Some were on balconies, others on stairs, others on rooftops. Then we saw a couple of rusted old buses full of people banging and yelling, rolling through red lights and careening about town. We didn't know what was going on, at least, not yet.

DAY EIGHT

We took a taxi to the airport, having made arrangements the night before, and flew north. When I got home, I read that there had been riots in Santo Domingo over a rise in the price of bread and basic foods, with 50 dead and 300 people injured, on the day that I had left.

7
VENEZUELA

I went to Venezuela around Christmastime one year. There were four of us: Pierre, who had been with me in Argentina and Chile, Odile, Raymonde, who was my companion in the Dominican Republic, and myself. Most of us had travelled in other Latin American countries, but in the past had shied away from Venezuela, with its notoriously high cost of living. Suddenly, with plunging world oil prices and the devaluation of the Bolívar, the country was affordable. We knew that with all the petroleum money of the past, there was a good road system, and without a large population, the situation looked good for biking. A cheap air fare was available, and we decided to take a closer look at Latin America's oil giant.

Venezuela is a large country, almost as big as France and Spain combined. The Andes run northeastward from Colombia toward the Caribbean coast, with peaks up to 5000 meters high. South of the mountains are tropical grassy plains, and forests and swamps. In the deep south, roads still do not penetrate parts of the Amazon jungle. On the coast and the offshore island of Margarita are beaches which are beginning to attract foreign visitors. Most people live on or near the coastal strip.

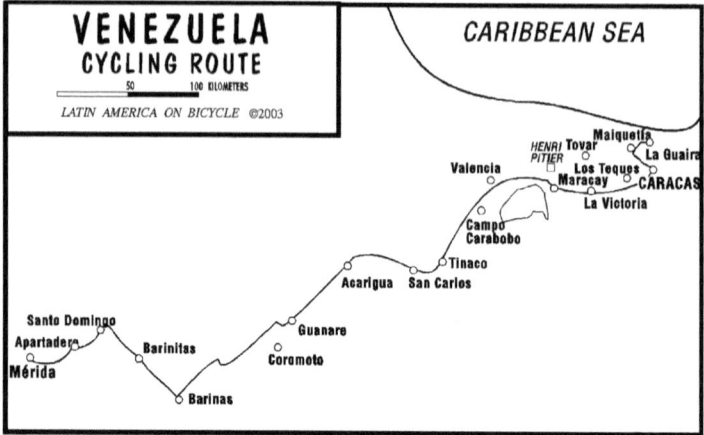

VENEZUELA CYCLING ROUTE

Venezuela has about 19 million people, and a per-capita income of about $4000, the highest in Latin America, thanks mainly to revenues from oil. The government oil company and state-sponsored enterprises are important players in the economy. Oil money has gone to build dams and steel complexes and roads, and pay for land-reform schemes.

Income and industrial statistics are deceiving, however. There are still plenty of poor people in Venezuela, though there are no desperate people, at least, not that we saw. Government social services provide a safety net. In Argentina, where income is much lower, people for the most part appear to live better. And the level of education is not up to that of, say, Costa Rica. Politically, Venezuela is stable, with a freely elected government, though dictators have ruled in the past.

Culturally, Venezuela is not as rich as many of its neighbors. There are pockets of indigenous peoples living traditionally, but no notable archeological sites. Until Venezuela became an oil exporter, the country was a poor backwater, known mainly for its Angostura bitters, Angel Falls, and jungles.

There are some unusual aspects to Venezuelan life. Locally grown coffee and a strong Italian influence have combined to make espresso- and capuccino-drinking extremely popular. Even at the end of the world, where people live in huts in the Amazon jungle, you can find a huge, hissing, steaming espresso machine, and for a couple of cents charge up with a thimbleful of liquid. It is quite good. And it is one of the few particularities of Venezuelan culture, I assure you.

Another is the cult of the automobile, which has developed in its own way. Gasoline costs a few cents a liter. When we rented a car, we didn't believe it when we filled the tank for a couple of dollars. Prices have since risen somewhat, as the government no longer forces the state oil company to dump production on the local market. But gas-guzzling piles of scrap remain on the road, and ample expressways have been built for them.

Then there is the immortal Simón Bolívar, liberator of the northern countries of South America. The money is the Bolívar, there is a city called Bolívar and you see Bolívar everywhere as a statue. There are also Bolívar Peak and as many Bolívar avenues and streets and parks as there are municipalities. I believe that the Bolívar cult must date from pre-petroleum times, when there was little else for Venezuela to toot about.

Well, these are oddities of Venezuela, but let me say that as far as biking goes, this is a good country for exploration. There are interesting sights and worthwhile experiences, and not just the natural attractions of the Amazon and the high Andes. Really, it's worth a visit to see the contrast of oil wealth and the rest. In Caracas there is a futuristic subway that cost zillions of dollars, next to the shacks of the poor. The roads are as good as there are anywhere in Latin America, the climate is benign, and there is sea, mountain, jungle, and whatever other landscape you care to choose.

We traveled for two weeks on bicycle, then rented a car for further exploration of areas that we would not have had time to see on bicycle. Quite frankly, we succumbed to the temptation of renting a car in an OPEC country where the price of gasoline was not a consideration.

While biking in Venezuela is rewarding, I would suggest doing things a little differently from how we did them. For one, you should be selective. Venezuela is big, so don't expect to see more than a few parts. The most interesting sections of the country are in the mountains of the states of San Cristóbal, Mérida and Trujillo, where roads are good, the grades are not demanding, traffic is light, scenery is magnificent, and there are good hotels. Because we did not give full consideration to the distances we would be covering, we spent days and days and days getting out of cities, and pedalling through essentially similar terrain until we reached this area. Let me tell you right off that if I go back—and I intend to—I will use planes and buses to get me and my bike to the mountains right off.

You could also concentrate your time near the coast, the beaches and the palms, though in this case you might want to land at Margarita or Puerto La Cruz. Maybe I'm too demanding, but I would be cautious about looking for sun and surf farther west. Beaches near Caracas, for miles and miles and miles, are not clean.

Also, there is a great potential for other sorts of exploration. You could go to the jungle, to the cowboy country of the plains, or on a combination bicycle-riverboat adventure.

You have to choose your roads carefully in Venezuela and exercise caution. Traffic is heavy near the cities and on the coast. Many roads are ill-cared-for by maintenance crews and the public in general. There are potholes into which you could practically disappear. I remember one that was full of water, which turned out to be a sewer manhole without its cover. Broken glass litters the streets around Caracas, and all of us had flat tires. Then there are dead dogs and all sorts of other obstacles. Never bicycle, or drive, for that matter, at night. You would not believe what you could hit.

Other than road safety, we had little concern for our personal security. The military is not overt in its presence. The police stopped us a couple of times to try to figure out what we were up to, but not in an unfriendly way. Really, Venezuela is a quiet country, and we never felt threatened or scared.

We rode touring bicycles, which were suited to the roads we took. Normal conditioning and ability will get you through a biking tour of Venezuela The sun is a problem, however. Bring plenty of protective lotion.

We didn't make any special preparations. Venezuela is rich enough to assure services and facilities. Corpoven, the state oil company, has maps available at its service stations. This, with the South American Handbook, was all we needed, though there were tourist brochures available in various places.

Bicycle stores exist in the larger towns. One was near the Hilton, where we stayed in Caracas. But you don't see talleres de bicicletas—bicycle repair shops—in all the small towns, the way you do in, say, Central America.

As you go south, you find yourself on roads with fewer facilities—hotels, restaurants, etc. Head to the jungle by all means if you're interested in birding and wildlife in general, but be prepared with ample food stocks, camping equipment, and malaria preventatives, and a mountain bike for the gravel and dirt roads. I've seen the roads from an airplane, they are mostly straight, and probably tiresome if you're down there pedalling.

We didn't take buses, it was in every way to our advantage to take a plane when we weren't biking. The cost was about double the bus fare.

The dry season is from December to April, though we ran into brief downpours on the coast and near Caracas. It was generally dry and warm, but not hot, at the lower altitudes in January. The mountains and the inland plains to the south are rainier. Bring the usual equipment, including sweater and gloves and hat for high altitude.

It was easy to buy food everywhere, and we didn't even bring a stove. But you have to be careful. All of us were sick from the food at one point or another. I myself was ill after eating a very good meal in the best hotel of Maracay. There is a local strain of malaria that is resistant to the usual preventative medications, for which one can take Fansidar by prescription.

Hotels were good, and clean, and we never had trouble finding a room, except when we arrived, which was on Christmas Eve.

Banks are efficient and pay the commercial rate for your money. Except for gas and transportation, and sometimes hotels, prices are about the same as in North America.

Air tickets to Venezuela can be reasonably priced—airplanes tank up in Venezuela for the return trip for next to nothing. We flew via New York, and our bikes arrived safely. More and more, as Venezuela attracts winter tourists, there are charter flights available to Puerto La Cruz and the island of Margarita.

Four was a good number for our group. In debates over which hotel to stay in or what road to take, more than four people would have been too many. With four, we had less weight: one repair kit, for example. When a repair was necessary, it went faster with everybody pitching in. When we all stayed in one room, it was cheaper. Security was better, with more eyes to keep on our belongings.

But there were some drawbacks. Sometimes one of us would lag behind and keep the others waiting, or somebody needed air, or somebody didn't feel well. And if we had taken buses, I think it would have been a disadvantage to have had four bicycles to load.

DAY ONE

It was a long trip. We arrived at 9:30 p.m., after leaving Montreal around 7 a.m., and stopping over for several hours in New York. It was obvious that the government had sunk money into Maiquetía airport, an ultramodern facility with electronic, ultrasonically activated doors. Because of the buildup to a strike at one of the airlines, it took several hours to extract our luggage. So we weren't on our way out of the terminal until midnight.

We looked around, there were taxis and also pickup trucks for hire, even at this hour. We chose the latter form of transportation for ourselves and our bikes. For about $15, the driver promised to find us a hotel. We piled in back with our bikes, and it began to rain, a heavy, heavy rain. The trip was not starting well.

The airport is near the beach north of Caracas, and there are many hotels. We looked at a good ten of them, until we ended up at a minimum, basic place near the main square of La Guaira, the port of Caracas. It was very clean, and the friendly owner agreed to keep the boxes for our bicycles until our departure.

The rain didn't last very long, maybe ten minutes, and it was quite warm, even in the middle of the night.

DAY TWO

We were up late, about 10:30, and with assembling our bicycles and loading our baggage, we weren't on the road until noon. We took the eight-lane boulevard along the sea, going west, and everything about it was disrepair. The street lights were broken, grass on the median strip grew to savage heights, repairs were in progress, dust was in the air, stores along the way were abandoned. And there was a lot of traffic headed toward the expressway to Caracas, a thousand meters higher.

We tried the expressway, but were barred from proceeding beyond the toll booths. We considered sneaking around, but the heavy truck and car traffic discouraged us from the adventure. So we backtracked to Maiquetía, where we easily found the old highway, the only other road going up into the mountains.

At the beginning, there were some slums alongside the road, shacks built on pillars on the mountainside—nothing could sit directly on that slope, and everything looks as if a good rain or a light push will send it to oblivion. I am sure that this is precisely what happens from time to time. But after a couple of kilometers, there were no more houses, and we were in the forest, on the nearly abandoned road. First the vegetation was quite dense, near sea level, like a jungle, then a more open forest. Cloud was forming above. The grade was not steep, there was no noise, and we looked down to Maiquetía, the airport runways, and the Caribbean stretching out beyond.

As we rose, we repeatedly ran into rock falls, small ones mostly, but some that nearly sealed the narrow road. No wonder drivers, even the uncautious, abandoned this scenery en masse when the new highway opened. Precisely one car passed us in 25 kilometers. It was fantastic for biking.

We reached the valley of Caracas, came out of the quiet, peaceful woods, and suddenly we were in shantytowns, full of people, noise, buses. The road was not bad, and we picked up speed for the five kilometers of slum to the city limits, just in case we looked like easy pickings for those not well off. There were holes, glass, assorted obstacles to pick our way around.

It took us about four hours from La Guaira to the capital, not counting a stop for lunch in Maiquetía. When we arrived, about 6 p.m., the sun was going down, the latitude being nearly equatorial.

Caracas was lively this Christmas day, there were lots of people in the streets, both well-off and poor-looking, and plenty of cars. Slums on the hills look down on a city center that is almost totally new, much of it built during the OPEC fat years.

We visited several hotels—we wanted a modern and comfortable one. We didn't want needless luxury, but since we were checking things out, we took a look at the Hilton Residencial. We could hardly believe the price—less than $30 for an apartment on two floors, with four bedrooms, three bathrooms, storage space for our bikes, washing machine, television, telephone, views, and the use of the pool and other facilities at the Hilton proper, next door. We looked no farther.

DAY THREE

Caracas is cool in the morning, pleasantly warm during the day, and cool again at night. We visited around the city, using the modern metro, or subway. Most official places of interest were still closed the day after Christmas, but we wandered the pedestrian malls and streets, and looked in the shops. Urban planning, or zoning, or something, was slightly cockeyed. A huge commercial complex of offices, apartments and retail space would be going up in the midst of slums. You leave a spanking-clean pedestrian street, and turn into a filthy alley populated by street hawkers.

We picked up information for a one-day tour to Canaima, a jungle city in the south. The day was getting on, the sun was going to set, so we rushed back to the Hilton to get some time in at the pool. We liked the facilities, and decided to stay another day in Caracas.

DAY FIVE

We took a taxi to Maiquetía to catch the early flight to Canaima. Our jet took us over the jungle in a flash, and soon set us down at an airstrip along the Caroní River, a tributary of the Orinoco.

We arrived to a strange landscape of tepuis, flat-topped mountains that look like the crown of a Spanish grandee's hat, rising out of the dense vegetation. Foaming rivers crash down in numerous falls, colorful flowers grow everywhere. We stayed at a cabin amid the foliage as part of our $100 package, there were few spiders and no snakes that I saw, and the meals were inoffensive. Budget travellers should not miss the opportunity to take a cheap flight and camp out.

Venezuela is especially rich in bird life, and some of the tepuis have their own unique species. There are almost always clouds in the rain forest at their tops.

We took some trips in dugout canoes. Excursions are also available to Angel Falls, the highest in the world with a thousand-meter drop. And there is an orchid preserve which is heaven for biologists.

Downriver is the huge Guri dam, which had a serious impact on the environment and the Indian life of the region. STOL planes made in Ontario buzz between the jungle village airstrips. With the Indian life, the dams and the sparse population, I found some similarities to northern Quebec, where I sometimes work. Except, of course, for the climate. Canaima was immortalized by Venezuelan novelist Rómulo Gallegos in a novel of the same name.

DAY SIX

We hiked up a small mountain near the runway, then flew back to Caracas and the Hilton Residencial. By this time, we had covered more distance by taxi and subway than by bicycle on our bicycle tour of Venezuela, but now we did our final planning for the road. We had originally considered going east along the coast, toward Barcelona, and over to Margarita Island. But from what we heard from others who had been that way, it would not have been too interesting a trip on bicycle. We decided instead to head toward the mountains.

DAY SEVEN

We should have left Caracas by bus, or taken a different route, but this is what we did: We were on the road about 1:30 p.m., and our progress was slow. We had to repair several flats—glass was everywhere on the streets. The thicker tires on mountain bikes would have been more resistant to this garbage.

We were headed for Los Teques, on one of the many excellent highways built with petrodollars. Traffic was heavy, which was due in part to the topography. Though Caracas occupies a fair-sized valley, access is through narrow passes, through which all traffic must funnel. We weren't going up or down, just squeezing between two mountains, with everyone else, in their cars. The way was lined with housing projects— Venezuelans are big on apartments for all social levels—and construction for a new metro line.

We didn't yet have a detailed road map, so it wasn't until later that we found out there was an alternative routing. I would recommend taking Highway 4, which is not a major road, in the direction of Tovar, climbing into the mountains. I went this way later, by car, and I can tell you that on bicycle it would have been fantastic. Tovar is a special place. It was settled in 1843 by Bavarian immigrants who brought along their printing press, brick kiln and tools. The atmosphere is Alpine, the climate is temperate, and everything is very clean. You can eat well and safely at a reasonable price, and there are numerous hotels. After a stay in Tovar, you can continue down on one of the best roads in Venezuela, a steep and well-maintained and scenic route, to Maracay. But this is what we didn't do.

We arrived in Los Teques, only 25 kilometers from Caracas, and checked in at the nearly empty Hotel Los Alpes, the largest in town, which is visible as you approach. Los Teques has little to interest visitors. We ate in the hotel restaurant on red captain's chairs, served by waiters in red, our plates set out on red tablecloths.

DAY EIGHT

We left early, traffic was still heavy, we passed Las Tejerías and La Victoria, the junction for Tovar. We followed the highway parallel to the main expressway, through a rugged landscape. If only there were fewer cars so that we could appreciate it better. The road was lined with trees as well as shanties. Somebody threw garbage over his fence and it landed on Pierre—orange peels and all. By 3 p.m. we were in Maracay, 72 kilometers from Los Teques.

We stayed at the Hotel Maracay, one of the best of our trip. For the four of us, the rate was about $40. It was about 15 minutes by bicycle from town, to the north, along a road lined with flowers. There was a nice pool. But watch out for the hotel dining room. I don't think it gets enough business, and the food goes off. I got sick. Maybe I was not lucky. I ate a veal cutlet with tomato sauce, one of my companions had just a taste of the sauce and became sick as well, but only a tenth of what I was.

We enjoyed the pool, but there was nothing special about the town. This is a dry area to the south side of the coastal range.

DAY NINE

We visited Henri Pitier Park, named for a French botanist, ten kilometers out of town on the highway north to the coast. It is an exuberant tropical forest, with zones of permanent fog and rain. There is another road northward to the coast at Independencia, where there are several good hotels. Maracay is high up, at 450 meters, and there is a mountain ridge to cross, so it would be a two-day round trip to the coast, or a full day if you go one way by bus.

Late in the day we headed west from Maracay, and cycled along the shore of polluted Lake Valencia. There was nothing special on the road we took, just a lot of cars, and, as we got to Valencia, shanties alongside. Traffic might have been lighter on the longer route around the south side of the lake. But in spite of the traffic, the temperature was ideal for bicycling, and it was dry and sunny, without wind.

Valencia is a place of money—cars are assembled there, and Venezuela is in love with cars. We went to the Intercontinental Hotel, and were received ungraciously. We leaned our bicycles against a concrete wall, and were promptly asked by a guard to leave. The price was about a hundred dollars, so we didn't want to stay there anyway, despite the lovely grounds. We decided instead for one of the many modest hotels in the town center.

People were friendly in Valencia, as elsewhere in the country. But Venezuelans were never curious about us, never got into conversations, just answered our questions and gave us directions politely.

DAY TEN

We left Valencia for Mérida, and had a choice of going by way of Barquisimeto, 200 kilometers to the west, by an up-and-down mountain road, or by a more circuitous but easier route southwest through the plains.

Our trip really began at Valencia. It should have begun at Caracas. But we made our mistakes, having not thought out our route carefully, and so until this day we had mostly been bicycling just for bicycling. Let me also tell you not to make the mistake of going north from Valencia. We travelled through this area by car, to several small ports on the edge of coastal swamps, and found little of interest.

We had to follow an expressway to the southwest, there was no alternative, but the shoulder was paved. The expressway came to an end at Campo Carabobo, 25 kilometers out, and a bit farther on was the Carabobo battlefield memorial, to Bolívar and a British soldier who had aided his cause. Everything in Venezuela is dedicated to Bolívar, but in this case it was not just one monument, but many monuments. It looked like the battle was still raging.

The road begins to be hilly, but mostly downhill toward the lowlands. We had a warm wind, and could see the great lowland expanse of the llanos. It was cattle country. Grass fires raged in places to clear the land. Traffic lightened up considerably. We reached Tinaco, on the plains, and the going was easy from there on.

In one day, we made it to San Carlos, about a hundred kilometers from Valencia. I was still a bit sick, and didn't look at the road too much, just concentrated on keeping up with the group.

Before and after each town is a Venezuelan kind of bus stop. It's more than a bus stop, really, a deluxe rest area with a filling station, restaurants, and stores selling everything you might need on the road, from chips to whiskey. And of course, you can have your capuccino. Whoosh. At one of these roadside villages, near San Carlos, a bus driver told us he had seen us for the last four days, twice a day, as he went back and forth on his route. He was happy, finally, to make our acquaintance.

The last stretch to San Carlos is wide and quiet, with mild ascents and descents. We arrived at sunset. San Carlos looked like a cowboy town—the locals favor wide-brimmed hats—and our bikes should have been transformed into horses. We stayed at the Hotel Central, which at the front looked really rundown and decrepit, made of dark, rotting wood painted brown. None of our group wanted to go in. But I explored through the swinging front doors, and found not a saloon, but a corridor leading to a modern hotel in back that looked just like an apartment building. It was managed by Italians, as are many hotels in Venezuela, and for about $8 per person we had a decent room, nice, clean and small, with a balcony and view of the town. We ate at the hotel, and I had to stick to soup for my still-nasty stomach. My companions enjoyed their meals.

DAY ELEVEN

Next morning, back in the saddle, we were off to Acarigua, 85 kilometers on. This was the only town where people were outgoing and friendly and stopped us to ask what it was like to cycle through their country. Our hotel, the Payara, sprawled on lush, landscaped acres, about 4 kilometers out of town on the Guanare road. The charge was about $10 each. Across the way, we dined on excellent local beef, washed down with a good red wine from Chile.

DAY TWELVE

My advice to you, if you go this way, is to take a bus from Acarigua to Barinas, a distance of 172 kilometers. We pedalled. The road was okay, except for some construction, but we were going through more and more of the same kind of country, and it was not worth the two days it took. The only notable site along the way was a church containing the relics of the Virgin of Coromoto, patron saint of Venezuela. In Guanare, we stayed at a decent hotel, the Portuguesa, for about $25 for all of us, and ate at a Middle Eastern restaurant—the sign outside was written in flowing Arabic script. We had noted other Arabic restaurants here and there in Venezuela. Signs round and about illustrated an insect and warned of Chagas disease, which is the same as African sleeping sickness. We saw one on the wall of a poor, mud-and-stick hut where we drank sodas while the barefoot kids of the household played in the dust. Some cotton fields provided relief from the landscape of cattle munching grass. It was dry, and we stopped often at roadside stands and stores to quench our thirst.

DAY THIRTEEN

We cycled past more cattle pastures, and people doing what they had to do. In Barinas, we looked for a hotel with a pool, and found two, but both were booked up, so we stayed in lesser surroundings at the Hotel Comercial, clean and plain and away from the main streets and noise. We ate in a Chinese restaurant, and all of us got sick during the night.

DAY FOURTEEN

We left in the morning with a food hangover. The only thing we had eaten in common was chop suey, so we knew what the culprit was, unless all the food was microbial.

We climbed from the llanos toward Barinitas, and this is where our trip began to get interesting. We went up, up and up. It was not really a long or difficult day, 40 kilometers, but in a short distance there was much to see, the landscape transformed before our eyes, as we ascended about 600 meters. There are large ravines, the vegetation gets greener, and there are longer and longer views down over the llanos. It was a bit like Vermont. And we could appreciate it all, as traffic was light.

We stayed in Barinitas. There was no point in continuing, it was a good day's trip to the next possible stopping point, Santo Domingo, another 50 kilometers on. The Hotel Lido, on the main road, was pleasant. The rooms are basic, simple, they give you a key but you can open the lock with your finger. We slept well.

DAY FIFTEEN

It was a very nice day travelling to Santo Domingo. In parts there are dangerous curves on this winding, climbing road, but it is beautiful, you can feel the mountain air as you ascend the cordillera, there are splendid views of huge canyons. Pierre at a certain point tried to take a picture while he was biking, and nearly went into one of them. At one of the warning signs—¡despacio!—a truck was perched on the edge, dumping its load of garbage into oblivion.

It is more and more cloudy as you go up, but not rainy— there is no worry about that. There are some falls, and the farming changes, as you enter a different country. People labored with oxen in the fields, but they did not have the look of impoverished peasants at this cool height. Their crops were potatoes and carrots and other produce known in the colder latitudes. The grade is constant at about four or five percent, You pass through the old-fashioned village of Las Piedras, take the left fork, and then you reach a good hill five kilometers long that takes you thirty minutes to get up before you enter Santo Domingo. We were there in six hours from Barinitas.

Santo Domingo was typical of the towns we were to come across in the state of Mérida, with thick-walled, plastered houses, huddled in a little valley, waterfalls tumbling down the surrounding slopes. The streams around are said to be good for trout fishing.

We stopped for the night at the Hotel Santo Domingo, four kilometers from the town center, an excellent establishment with good food and service. Horseback riding is available from the hotel. The price was less than $10 per person. There are several other good hotels, including the Hotel Los Frailes, in the center, which is a converted monastery. It has an reputation for excellence, and reservations are required well in advance.

DAY SIXTEEN

We stopped for breakfast at Cafetería Las Tapias, then entered the paramo, an area of the very special type of vegetation of high tropical altitudes. Typical are frailejones, members of the dandelion family which grow several feet tall. From Santo Domingo, the road goes up, up and up. You cross a pass over 4000 meters above sea level. It became cloudier and cloudier. But we pedalled eagerly toward the summit, in anticipation of the views.

When we reached the top, the clouds broke, it was sunny. Right there, at the junction for Apartadero, we had an excellent roadside meal, a stew with local potatoes, at a restaurant next to a trout lake. The place was full of tourists, most of them from Venezuela, and many of them wearing woolen hats like mine.

Apartadero snuggles beneath mountain ridges. On one of them is a series of four observatories of the University of the Andes in Mérida. There are several small hotels, all white with red tile roofs, and all looking quite acceptable. It was mid-afternoon, we still had 60 kilometers to go to Mérida, people told us it was downhill all the way. But we should have stopped, for even going down, down, down it takes hours to cover 60 kilometers. We were not cars.

Just as we set out again, a group of young people on horses appeared from a mountain trail and tried to race us. What a contest! We crouched close to our handlebars, lifted our feet. Before we could start pedalling we had coasted to victory. Along the roadside, a vendor hawked boiled papas del paramo—the local potatoes have a just fame. The vendor stood motionless. I asked him about his business, he said that one car had stopped that day. It was quite cold, and yet, he didn't move, though he was lightly dressed.

We put on our woolen hats and gloves for the descent. It was good bicycling, the slope was gentle, the views were fantastic, the best of the trip, of narrow valleys meandering down and away, rustic churches, terraced hillsides.

The last ten kilometers from Tabay to Mérida were not downward at all, however. The sun set at six o'clock, the road was suddenly busy, and it rained. At night, it was dangerous. We arrived after 9 p.m., and were very tired. We checked several hotels, at this hour they were already full. We finally registered at the Hotel Plaza, a regular, clean, friendly place. We were pointed to it by some French people we met on a street.

Mérida is one of the nicest Latin American towns I have seen, situated on a long plateau. There are good restaurants, and a university. You meet lots of interesting people there, they look intelligent and educated. There is no squalor. A lot of money looks to have been invested to make this a nice place in which to live and study. The restaurants are clean, the phones work, there are good hotels. Especially recommendable for eating are the empanadas.

DAY SEVENTEEN

We toured the town, and I was quite impressed. The illusion of a colonial city is given by the uniform style of whitewashed walls and red tile roofs. Parks are spotless, shaded from the mountain sun by palm trees.

We took the longest and highest cable car ride in the world, over an hour and a half to cover 12 kilometers to the top of Pico Espejo, 4700 meters above sea level. You can't stay more than an hour, or exert yourself at all, or you will get a splitting headache. We felt lucky to make it. You know, in South America, you are always a little bit scared. We wondered how often the line had been inspected since opening in 1959, probably as a petro-project. We had to go early in the morning. The peak is always clear, but the valley fills with clouds in the afternoon.

After visiting the university and wandering around town, we went to the airport. Our biking trip stopped at Mérida, though with more time it would have been a good idea to continue to San Cristóbal, 263 kilometers to the southwest, through more of the Andes. There was no point in taking a bus back to Caracas, when the air fare was $25 in a large jet. You ride the highway out to the airport, buy your ticket—there is no problem getting a seat—then pedal out to the plane, hand over your bicycle to the baggage handlers, climb up, and an hour later you're in Maiquetía, hassle-free.

8
ARGENTINA AND CHILE

Here are two countries that, for biking purposes, I'll consider together. There are a few reasons for this.

You can perfectly well bicycle only in Chile or only in Argentina. But some of the most interesting parts of both countries are in the Cordillera de los Andes, the great mountain spine that separates the two republics. If you go up into the cordillera from Chile, sooner or later you'll find yourself in Argentina, and vice versa.

There are lots of other places than the cordillera in Argentina, the seventh largest nation in the world. But for travelling in Chile, a string bean of a country dominated by the Andes, Argentina makes a useful alternative route. In parts, Chile is hardly wider than a single highway. That highway carries all the north-south traffic, naturally, with little room for safe cycling. And even if you use public transport to carry you part of the way, you might want to cross to Argentina to avoid retracing your route.

We arrived in Argentina in late December one year, just as a civilian government was displacing the military. The heavy hand of authoritarian rule seemed to have evaporated. We saw hardly any soldiers, and even policemen were few. Despite the recent Falklands war and repression at home, and territorial disputes with all of its neighbors, Argentina at the time of our visit was emphatically at peace. We only felt tension, and military presence, at the borders. On the other hand, in Chile, the army and the carabineros—the national police—were everywhere.

Argentina is not like most Latin American countries. Buenos Aires has more in common with Paris or Madrid than with Bogota: wide boulevards, well-groomed parks, and even a subway. Once one of the wealthier countries, after the 1920s Argentina's fortunes declined. Nevertheless, with a small population of 30 million, and ample resources, its potential is great. People are generally literate and educated. Many spoke to us quite well in French, as well as English. Spain, Italy and Germany were major sources of immigrants after independence, and our impression was of a country that would have fit well somewhere in southern Europe.

Argentina is continental in scale, ranging from the glaciers and taiga of Tierra del Fuego to desert to the rich grasslands of the pampas to steaming tropics in the north. Argentines have a strong sense of nationalism. Like Australians, they are removed in distance from North Americans and Europeans with whom they feel somewhat in sympathy, and have their own idiosyncrasies.

Chile is noticeably poorer than Argentina, somewhere in the middle level among Latin American nations. The country is safe for a visitor getting around by bicycle. Aside from the ever-visible Andes, the landscape varies from fertile valleys at the center to the barren and mineral-rich Atacama desert of the north to the fjord country of the south. In general, the farther south you go, the rainier and windier it is.

Perhaps the most striking thing about the climate in Argentina and Chile is the inversion of seasons. When it's winter in the northern hemisphere, it's summer down there. We went during the southern summer, of course, and found the temperature warm inland and at low altitudes, and cool in

CENTRAL
ARGENTINA & CHILE
CYCLING ROUTE
25   50 KILOMETERS
LATIN AMERICA ON BICYCLE ©2003

the mountains. The waters off the coast and the sea breezes are cool, however. Don't expect to do much sunbathing.

For the cyclist, scenery is the main harvest in both Argentina and Chile. Mountains are as high as you'll see anywhere outside of Asia. Notable wildlife in Argentina includes species of penguins seen nowhere else. In the Andes, archeological sites contain important and fascinating monuments of Inca civilization. In both countries, there are pockets of indigenous people living traditional lives, well off the beaten track.

The quality of roads is a big plus for the cyclist in Argentina. Construction standards are similar to those of the United States, and better than Canada's. Outside of the larger cities, traffic is light. In Chile, roads are not up to Argentine standards, but for Latin America, they are quite good. Drivers are civilized. When we met up with a car or truck, the driver would flash his lights in greeting and solidarity, rather than blasting his horn, which is the custom in some other parts of Latin America.

Distances are long in these countries, even if you are selective, as we were. And there are climatic peculiarities that make the going tough in parts. We found, by checking a meteorological atlas beforehand, that there would be strong west winds blowing up into the Andes, especially in the south.

Accordingly, we planned a west-to-east crossing from southern Chile. We briefly faced a severe head wind when crossing into Chile, and freak winds near the Valdés Peninsula, in Argentina.

Even though the grades are not too difficult, moderate ability and conditioning are required.

Aerolíneas Argentinas gave us a general tourist map of Argentina, which includes Chile as well. This is adequate for orientation. The Automóvil Club Argentino publishes detailed maps of each Argentine province. These are available at club offices in large cities. In Chile, good regional maps and guides—the Guía de Viaje Bancosorno series—are sold at bookstores. Tourist offices also supply maps.

With vast spaces to choose from, we ruled out long, straight journeys through the pampa and desert. We also eliminated Patagonia, with its rocky landscape and winds. We actually made three separate tours, and used public transport in between.

We found that it was every bit as difficult to get our bikes onto buses in Argentina as in North America. Trains were less of a problem, and it was quite easy to load our bikes onto airplanes, and there was no charge.

It is, of course, helpful to speak Spanish, but in Argentina, and to a lesser extent Chile, English, French, and even German are understood.

Our touring bicycles, with eighteen speeds and normal tires, were adequate throughout our trip. We could have made it on twelve-speed bikes, though we would have encountered problems in the mountains. On only one day did we cycle a gravel road on which a mountain bike would have been preferred.

Weather in the Argentine and Chilean summer is generally similar to that in June and July in the northern United States and southern Canada. A generous amount of sunscreen is required.

We ate well in both Argentina and Chile. Even though I eat tofu at home, I couldn't pass up the fresh, succulent, inexpensive beef in Argentina. I ate steak twice a day. Both countries have fine, inexpensive domestic red wines— Argentina is the largest wine producer in the southern hemisphere. Tap water is generally safe, but good mineral water is available everywhere as well.

One of the peculiarities of Argentina and Chile is yerba mate tea, usually consumed through a pipe from a gourd vessel. A charge of yerba mate will keep you going all day.

We generally had breakfast at our hotels. With no worries about the safety of the food, we didn't take a portable stove, though economy travellers might want to bring one.

Hotels in Argentina are absolutely the best I have seen for the price (though a firming exchange rate has since decreased this advantage). There are plenty of them, catering mostly to domestic tourists. At the time of our visit, prices for food and lodging were about a third lower in Argentina than in North America, and lower still in Chile. Hotels seemed to be more crowded after January 7, when the summer vacation period starts. I don't see any necessity, pricewise, to take camping equipment.

We flew Aerolíneas Argentinas from Montreal to Buenos Aires, with no change of plane. For no additional fare, we then boarded another flight, for Mendoza, at the foot of the Andes. There are many flights to Buenos Aires from New York and Los Angeles as well.

DAY ONE

In New York, we were ushered into a windowless transit room, where we had to stay for two hours. Our bikes remained on the plane, as we had a through flight. In Rio, things were a bit better. We could walk around the airport, drink coffee, mail postcards. The customs inspector at Ezeiza Airport in Buenos Aires was concerned that we might sell our bikes. We told him we were entered in a carrera—a race—and he waved us through, happy to make our acquaintance.

We were put on a bus for the Aeroparque, the domestic airport, and by the afternoon of December 18, 26 hours out of Montreal, we were in the airport in Mendoza. We assembled our bicycles, and headed into the what a tourist brochure calls the "land of sun, snow and good wine."

Immediately, we lost our bearings. Road signs told us to go one way to downtown Mendoza, our instincts told us to go the opposite way. We looked at a map, puzzled, until we realized that in the southern hemisphere, the sun was on the wrong side of the sky at midday—the north.

We cycled to downtown in an hour. The first thing we did was have a meal, at a restaurant on the wide Avenida San Martín. We could have been at a café-terrasse in southern France, looking out on the boulevard, watching well-dressed people promenade in front of the cafés and bars. We ate steak—steak in one form or another was practically all there was on the menu—and then set out to find a hotel. We looked at about eight of them, and settled for the Crillón, a perfectly adequate establishment on Avenida Perú west of the main square. The tab was $15 double. There are several similar establishments on the streets nearby. In the bathroom, I had my introduction to Argentine plumbing. When I turned the handle in the tub, water squirted up from the bottom, like a little fountain.

DAY TWO

We arose quite late, about 11 a.m., having slept off our plane trip. We wanted to visit the natural history museum on Plaza Independencia, but it was closed. The tourist office gave us reams of information. This is a skiing, hiking, and general vacation area for Argentines, with numerous good accommodations, wineries, and historic sites to visit. Several loop trips of two or three days from Mendoza are possible. We had a choice of two routes up into the Andes toward Chile, one to the north and then west, over a partly unpaved road, via the thermal springs at Villavicencio, where there is a famous old-fashioned hotel; the other to the south and then west and north, meeting the first route at Uspallata, 105 kilometers from Mendoza. We planned to take the southern route, and spend the first night at the resort hotel in Potrerillos, only 50 kilometers distant.

But first we rode up to Cerro de la Gloria, a hill in a park overlooking the city from the west. At the summit is a monumental statue of Gen. San Martín winning yet another victory in the struggle for independence. Views of the area are impressive. We could see that Mendoza lay in the desert, but with irrigation water from the mountains, cultivation of grapes was widespread.

Back in town, we consumed steak and wine, and watched the day pass on the Avenida San Martín. And watched and watched. By the time we left Mendoza, it was mid-afternoon. And that was a mistake. Getting to Potrerillos is a full day's excursion.

The road from Mendoza was flat and straight to Godoy Cruz, just a few kilometers to the south, and beyond toward Boites. In the distance, beyond the flat expanses, we could see the precordillera, the lower range that runs along the looming main spine of the Andes.

And then, at 7 p.m., it was dark, even though it was summer. We were at about 33 degrees south, as far from the equator as Los Angeles. At this latitude, we would not experience the long evenings of the early Canadian summer.

By the dim light of a half moon, we ascended into the precordillera, which we would traverse for the next two days, gradually climbing, dropping occasionally, but encountering no significant mountain grades as we followed the canyon of the Mendoza River. Traffic was light, a truck passed perhaps every twenty-five minutes. Though there were no incidents, it was not the safest time to be on the road.

The views of the Andes, even in moonlight, were fantastic. In the higher stretches now, beyond the reach of irrigation, the land was desertic.

We got to Potrerillos after 11 p.m., ready to hit the sack, only to discover that every room in the rustically designed mountain lodge was taken by a convention of dentists! We asked around to see if we could find a room in a private house, there was nothing, only a campsite. So we spent the night on park benches, dozing fitfully, cold, without sleeping bags.

DAY THREE

We were up early in the park, of course, about 6 a.m., and set out immediately. The sun rose, soon it was warm. Snow-capped Cerro El Plata, to the south, 6000 meters high, rose over us as we headed northwest, up through the barren, rocky slopes of the precordillera. About a kilometer out of Potrerillos, past the intersection for the road to Vallecitos, we stopped and perked ourselves up with a breakfast of eggs and ham and tomatoes at a roadside restaurant. Pierre, my companion, replaced a spoke that had broken the previous evening, during our search in the dark for accommodations. This was our only mechanical problem of the entire trip.

At this point, despite the magnificent vistas all around, we were out of it. What sleep we had had over the previous days had not been sufficient.

Our climb was gradual, and without incident.

It was warm, but on this day I covered myself with long pants and long sleeves. We had not put on enough sun cream the previous day, and had cooked like lobsters. We were experiencing total sun, as I have rarely experienced it anywhere else. The peaks that spread out before us for dozens—and later, as we rose, for hundreds—of kilometers, were entirely free of clouds. At night, in the clear mountain air, we had viewed the Southern Cross, and a carpet of millions of stars. The constellations were all unfamiliar to me.

About 30 kilometers out of Potrerillos, we stopped at a restaurant for a snack. Before 2 p.m. we crossed the Mendoza River on a steel bridge that in the bright sunlight seemed to be made of pure silver, and were in Uspallata, 60 kilometers from Potrerillos. Here we were at the end of the precordillera, ready to start up into the Andes proper.

And here we had a disagreement. Pierre wanted to continue. Our map showed places ahead along the road—Picheuta, La Cortadera, Polvaredas, Punta de Vacas. Surely there would be accommodations in some of them, and we still had daylight. But I was tired, and wanted to stop and take it easy while we were ahead. I stood my ground.

Uspallata is a dry little town with earthen streets, a post office, several shops, and a garage—useful, perhaps, for repairs—backdropped by the snow-capped Andes. We stayed at the Hotel Uspallata, an old-fashioned place redolent of past glories. Large public rooms and old writing tables bespoke a time when getting to this place was an expedition.

We had to air out our damp panelled room, but as usual we ate well. The gymnasium-sized dining room was furnished like a museum, and we looked onto an artfully landscaped English garden, with trees and flowers, statuary, and modest bridges over a little stream. The price of this luxury was about eight dollars each. We stocked up in town with food for the next day, and slept well.

DAY FOUR

A sign outside of Uspallata indicates when the road is closed by snow in winter. We followed the Mendoza River, mostly dry after the spring snow melt, now climbing on a more pronounced grade. Numerous rock tunnels took us through slopes too steep for construction of a surface road.

The highway was provided in places with a slow lane for rare ascending trucks. Several truckers stopped, and offered to take us and our bikes aboard. We declined, but it was reassuring to know that we could have had a lift if necessary. There were few cars, and occasionally, a convoy of four or five buses would pass.

Along the way, the old Sendero de los Incas—the Inca Trail—crosses the modern highway, just past La Cortadera. Several large stone buildings remain at the point where the trail comes to the Río Mendoza. The trail ran from Peru to Patagonia, through the Andes all the way.

Beyond the "junction" of the Inca Trail, the road rises sharply. We found that we—I?—had been wise to stop in Uspallata for the night. There was nothing, or next to nothing, in the way of settlement. The names on the map were only wide spots, with a building or two, a ski center shut down for the summer, and no accommodations.

At Punta de Vacas we found a large military base, this being a sensitive border region, and went through immigration formalities. It is essential not to omit this step, or you'll be sent back down from the border—a loss of at least a day. The reward is an attractive stamp. After Punta de Vacas, the road follows the rail line to Santiago. Passenger trains no longer run. We could see Puente del Inca, above us and six kilometers distant. But due to the Venturi effect—winds speeding up as they rushed through the constricted mountain pass from Chile in the early afternoon—we plodded along in the lowest of 18 gears. The grade was not as great as elsewhere, but it took us more than an hour to get up to Puente del Inca.

We arrived about 5 p.m., having left Uspallata at 10 a.m. It's a good idea when cycling this road to get an early start. You can cover more distance in one hour in the morning than in several hours in the afternoon. The wind turned off in the evening—just like that—and it was quiet after seven o'clock.

Puente del Inca—Inca Bridge—is spectacular. A natural rock bridge spans the tributary of the Río Mendoza that carved it out over the centuries. Abutting it are thermal baths built by more recent inhabitants. We entered the bathing rooms, carefully, and took a bath in tepid spring water flowing in from the bottom. Above the baths, spring water seeps into pools that smell slightly of sulphur.

A hotel here had been destroyed by an avalanche—its ruins are still visible. We stayed in a newer, modern one, Hostería Puente del Inca, built—I hoped—in a more secure spot, next to yet another military base. Signs warned us not to take pictures—no doubt Chilean spies frequent this road. The hotel was the highest place we stayed at, and also highest in price, but worth it. There are, in fact, no other acceptable accommodations between here and the border. In the summer it was not busy—the hotel exists mainly for skiers, some of them Chilean, whose own resorts have fallen on hard times.

The next day, just beyond Puente del Inca, we could see snow-capped Aconcagua to the north, at 7035 meters the highest peak in the Americas, and in the southern hemisphere as well. We could almost reach out and touch this giant, though it was a good twenty kilometers distant. Expeditions to Aconcagua leave from Puente del Inca, and are always accompanied by a military escort. The Alpine Club in Mendoza is helpful in arranging all the details. We met a returning Japanese expedition at our hotel. Less challenging climbs and hikes are available in the area as well.

DAY FIVE

We left Puente del Inca early, determined to avoid another encounter with head wind. A three-car train huffed and chugged alongside us part of the way, headed to a mine. In four hours we made it up to Las Cuevas, 25 kilometers distant, through mountains colored ochre, olive, and sand.

At Las Cuevas, the road divides, one branch climbing another 300 meters to a pass, the newer route taking a more level course toward a tunnel. We stopped for a good meal in a bus converted to a diner, then headed for the tunnel, leaving what was, all in all, the most pleasant cycling road I had ever been on. We had risen about 3000 meters from Mendoza, over a road distance of 200 kilometers, and despite bouts with wind, the climb had been benign. On another occasion, in Costa Rica, I was to climb a similar height in only 25 kilometers of road.

At the tunnel entrance a sign declared that the Malvinas—the Falkland Islands—belong to Argentina, war results notwithstanding. We were waved through the toll gate.

The tunnel, about 3.5 kilometers long and curving in a semicircle, was a joint effort of Argentina and Chile. The slope from our side was downward—about a three percent grade. We raced through, to keep cars and trucks from overtaking us in the narrow roadway. The Argentine side was well maintained and lit, but halfway through, we didn't know what had hit us. The lights went out. Water seeped through the walls onto a rutted surface. We splashed through and nearly had several spills. A truck reverberated somewhere behind us. We pedalled furiously, and suddenly popped out into the daylight of Chile.

The official entry point to Chile is five kilometers past the end of the tunnel. There it took us an hour to go through formalities. It wasn't unpleasant—there was a good restaurant. Our bicycles required a form in triplicate, with due notation of our license plates. I don't know if we would have made it through without them. We changed some money here as well.

From the customs post you go down, down, down on your brakes. You see almost immediately that you are in another country, even though the land is basically the same. Chile is not as up-to-date as Argentina, and is noticeably poorer.

We levelled out past a deep blue lake in a mountain fissure, and the dormant ski center of Portillo.

Beyond, the road descended again, not in the gradual way of the well-constructed Argentine roads, but in ribbons of poorly maintained asphalt and concrete winding back and forth on cliff faces. At 2 p.m., on schedule, the wind appeared to buffet us. We bumped and bounced our way over concrete slabs, slowing down repeatedly to keep control. Our brakes smoked, and we stopped for stretches of five and ten minutes so that the heat would not explode our tires. We could feel the air becoming noticeably warmer. Soldiers at several military bases along the way stood ready to repel an Argentine attack.

We rolled into Río Colorado at 4 p.m., and checked into the small and clean Hotel Río Colorado, which is used as a summering spot by Santiago's German community. Rooms in back, away from early-morning truck noise, are preferable. The trucks take workers up to a mine—we saw them return in the afternoon full of men in helmets. Near the town is a hydroelectric dam. We ate and slept well, after a good day's run.

DAY SIX

Descending from Río Colorado, more gradually, the road was quiet. Its condition improved as it traversed a landscape of cactus and low bushes. Los Andes, on the edge of the central valley, was the first town of any size that we entered. It has a bank, a pleasant central park, and a mañana air.

We followed the major highway south, through the narrow Chacabuco Tunnel. On bicycle, it was dangerous—traffic presses you against the tunnel wall for one kilometer. A reflective safety vest is needed. The slope is still downward to the tunnel; then past it, for 60 kilometers or so, the land is flat all the way to Santiago. Along the way are several military bases, the modernistic Monumento a la Victoria, and a NASA satellite-tracking station.

None of which is very interesting. If I were doing this trip over, I would continue from Los Andes to the coast, down the valley of the Aconcagua River, to Valparaíso and Viña del Mar. This would have added a day, and allowed us some beach time. But the gravity of the capital pulled us, and we followed the main line of traffic.

We were proceeding on our way past a military base, all innocence, when we were motioned to stop. In Chile, when the military is in control (as it was at the time), you follow orders. Pierre was interrogated closely. Where was he from? What was he doing? When they realized they had captured a couple of Canadians, the soldiers let us go.

The problem was Pierre's hat, which he had bought in Uspallata. Light blue and white, it displayed too blatantly the colors of Argentina.

At Esmeralda, we passed a large, sandbagged police post, and continued onto a wide boulevard toward Santiago. We were in the sprawling capital at 3 p.m., having left Río Colorado at 9:30 a.m.

The center of the city is full of hotels, and we found lodging with no problem on a pedestrian mall, so the hotel was quiet, as well as cheap.

Traffic was heavy, and the most advisable thing was to leave our bicycles in our hotel room. It was almost Christmas, and street photographers offered to take Polaroid shots of us with Santa Claus in a sled pulled by two llamas.

Currency exchange confounded us less in Chile than in Argentina, where we had been given pesos, old pesos, and older pesos. It was easy to change money on the street in both countries, at better than the official rate, and in Argentina, even some banks paid the black-market rate if nothing was written down.

In Chile, the black market was more obviously illegal. On one street corner, a tough-looking fellow with huge arms solicited our exchange business, then took out a pocket calculator, but his beefy index finger kept pressing too many tiny touch pads. Two policemen appeared, and our money merchant put his hands behind his back, rocked on his heels,

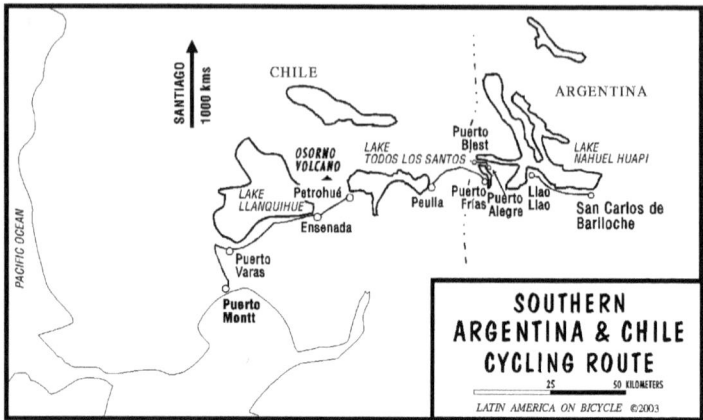

SOUTHERN
ARGENTINA & CHILE
CYCLING ROUTE

LATIN AMERICA ON BICYCLE ©2003

whistled innocently, and looked guilty as hell. When we asked him what the problem was, this bulldog of a man rumbled back: "*porque . . . este . . . es . . . un . . . país . . . de . . . mierda.*" And the twenty-percent premium he paid for our dollars indicated that things were not looking so good for the economy that day.

Everywhere in Chile the air is not of a poor Latin American country, but of a country that has fallen on hard times. The roads are in disrepair, the vehicles are old and kept patched and running, clothes are neat but threadbare. Soldiers and checkpoints are everywhere.

DAY SEVEN

We spent one full day in Santiago. Military buses rolled up and down the streets, their windows grated, machine guns mounted on top. Troops marched through the streets, arresting street vendors who could not pack up quickly enough, and generally intimidating people. There are shanty towns all around the outskirts of the capital, but the downtown area is modern. There are pleasant parks, and monumental edifices for the post office and the then-dormant chamber of deputies. In the evening we left for Puerto Montt.

Our Ferrocarril del Sur train departed at 6 p.m. and arrived in Puerto Montt, a thousand kilometers to the south, at 11 the next morning. The fare was less than $30, dormitorio (sleeper) class, which included dinner, breakfast and sleeping berth. Our only problem was our bicycles. This train was for passengers only, and by the usual procedures, we would have had to send our bicycles aboard another train that would arrive half a day later.

But I am firm in the principle of never leaving your bicycle, if at all possible. With a tip here, a tip there, a discussion here, and a heated argument there, we managed to put our bicycles to bed in a compartment next to ours.

We travelled in old English coaches, built around 1950, finished entirely in wood. We were served by men uniformed like penguins, to recorded fifties music coming out of scratchy speakers, as the train clicked and clacked. For a $2 supplement, we were privileged to enjoy a whiskey and the on-board cinema in the bar car. The movie, following a whiskey, was funny, I think. Obviously, in Chile, the train is still the way to go.

DAY EIGHT

We had breakfast aboard, and when we pulled into Puerto Montt, we were refreshed and ready to go.

We could have gotten off the train at Puerto Varas, 17 kilometers before Puerto Montt, at the junction for our trans-Andean route over the mountains and across several lakes (by boat, not bike). But we wanted to get a look at Puerto Montt, a good-sized city on a fjord-like sea arm, in an area set aside by the Chilean government for German colonization in the last century. Here, in Chile's lake region, rain is heavy, but on our first day there was not a cloud in the sky.

Any number of circular excursions from Puerto Montt are possible on the roads that fan out into the Alpine landscape. To the south, the Pan American Highway is interrupted by fjords and mountains plunging to the ocean edge, but steamers provide service down to Punta Arenas near the bottom of the world (or I should say top, as that's where our map showed the South Pole), as well as to other inhabited points in what is mostly a no man's land.

Vegetation around Puerto Montt is similar to that of the more temperate regions of Canada. The influence of the sea is everywhere. Dozens of little stores around the harbor sell fresh fish, and red, blue and green sea denizens, the likes of which I had never seen in a supermarket. My stomach didn't want to explore, but Pierre consumed several of these red, blue and green creatures, which the keeper of an eatery consented to cook for one minute—usually they're eaten raw.

We left for Puerto Varas—a port on Lake Llanquihue, not the sea—and it took us about two and a half hours to cover the flat 25 kilometers in the wind. And there Pierre nearly died.

As in Puerto Montt, the constant wind and the clustered houses and boats gave the air of a Maine seaport to the town. Only the volcanoes that towered to the east were really different. They retain a permanent cap of snow, though they are only about 2500 meters high, and about as far from the equator as Mt. Washington in New Hampshire. They are not difficult to climb. Vegetation is lush from the heavy rains.

We stayed at the Gran Hotel Puerto Varas, on Calle Klenner, a huge, nearly luxurious hotel where the rate was about $10 per person. The place had seen better days, but the management was making an effort to keep up in difficult times, though we had the feeling of being in a great haunted house. Geriatric ladies waited on us, dressed like comic-strip Hazel, with tiny caps. The casino was nearly empty but for some players who might have been cloned from creations of Charles Addams. I performed an important experiment in the bathtub, having been informed that the rotation of water going down a drain was in the opposite direction from that in the northern hemisphere. Three times the water went clockwise, twice it went counterclockwise. So I did not arrive at a definitive conclusion.

As for Pierre . . . It was the fish, or whatever the sea creatures were, that nearly did him in. He writhed and sweated on his bed, and shook in convulsions, victimized by a gastro-intestinal poisoning. I gave him a medicine that helped not at all.

DAY NINE

We had breakfast in our hotel room, and left in a rainstorm. Lake Llanquihue was a cauldron of waves. Lashed by the wind, we had to tack from side to side in order not to be blown off our bikes. We were headed toward Petrohué, 66 kilometers distant, the port for a ferry across Lake Todos Los Santos.

Pierre's stomach was still suffering, though he bravely pedalled on, exhausted as he was. His stomach was delicate for several days, until he consulted a doctor in Bariloche, who prescribed antibiotics.

The lakeside road was lined with small cattle and dairy farms, and also, in this vacation area, with restaurants. We ate steaks cooked over a wood fire at Río Blanco, then proceeded to Ensenada, the junction for the road to Petrohué. Our cycling time was about three and half hours from Puerto Varas.

Ensenada has several hotels, and there are others in Petrohué, and it would be quite practical to stay in this region a few days, setting out on foot, perhaps, for the summit of one of the volcanoes. A secondary road from Ensenada ascends onto the slopes of the volcano Osorno. There are several hot springs as well.

From Ensenada, the road is unpaved to Petrohué. Our tires squished into the rain-softened surface. Eventually, the rains let up, and we could see the magnificent country we were traversing. At Saltos de Petrohué we gazed at the Petrohué river crashing down in a series of rocky falls, and climbed up for a view of the volcanoes from a new perspective.

At Petrohué, a town with many log houses, we stopped at the Swiss-run Hostal Petrohué—there are lots of Swiss and Germans in the hospitality business in southern Chile—and ate Torte, a German-style pie. It was excellent after a bicycle trip, and a break from steak. We drank tea and dried out, then at 4 p.m. boarded the ferry that took us across mountain-rimmed Lake Todos Los Santos to Peulla, where we arrived at 6:30 p.m. There are only a couple of daily departures. These steamers are also used to shuttle cattle from one rich lakeside pasture to another.

There is a large motel in Peulla, and rooms are rented out in private homes. It makes a good place to stop for the night, if you have not spent the evening in Petrohué. By no means should a cyclist attempt an afternoon climb up to the Argentine frontier.

We stopped by the large, mountain-style motel and chatted with the Swiss owner in German. He asked a price for a room which we felt was a bit high—he had a near-monopoly. Somebody else took us to see a room in a private house, which turned out to be dirty and run-down, and expensive as well. Then we went back to the hotel, where the owner made a better price. The family that ran the hotel also controlled the dam that generated electricity for the town, and had an arrangement to provide dinner to all tour-bus passengers.

DAY TEN

A kilometer out of Peulla is the immigration control point, where we had our passports stamped. Beyond, we continued up the valley of the Peulla River, past numerous large farms. Over a flat stretch of two kilometers, as we passed through pastures, we were set upon by cattle flies. Ten kilometers out of Peulla, all of it unpaved and narrow—really, this was just a country road—we came to a second checkpoint. Beyond, the road climbs 1200 meters to the pass at the border, through slopes of forest and meadow. Rocks in the road, and the slope, forced us to dismount and push our bikes. With wider tires, we might have been able to pedal. Fortunately, the weather held. The wind, as the meteorological books had promised us, was at our backs.

A sign at the top of Pérez Rosales pass—nothing else— informed us that we were in Argentina. We paused, of course, to appreciate the fact, then we rolled down a few kilometers to Puerto Frías.

A road runs southeast from Puerto Frías, then northeast to the Argentine lake resort town of San Carlos de Bariloche. But the short route is by ferry, road, ferry and road again.

We went through immigration procedures, said hello to some hikers, took note of the usual detachment of soldiers on frontier alert, and had just enough time to catch the ferry across green Lake Frías, bordered by snow-flecked slopes. It might have been Lake Louise in Alberta. A dirt road at the other end, memorably scenic, led us in fifteen minutes to Puerto Blest, where there is a hotel. We ate dinner looking out on the western arm of Lake Nahuel Huapi, and the huge trees that grow on this side of the cordillera, where the climate is drier than in Chile. Then we boarded the lake steamer.

We ended up at a little port that I thought was called Llao Llao. The Argentines around me on the boat knew nothing about it. They said we were going to Jao Jao. I showed them Llao Llao on the map, they insisted it was Jao Jao, and I learned a lesson in Argentine pronunciation.

On the road again at Llao Llao, or Jao Jao, we headed toward Bariloche, through Argentina's premier resort country, a cool summering spot, and a ski area in winter. I felt that I was once again in the mountains north of Montreal—the same roads rising and falling on the hillsides, the same rocky country dotted with lakes. We passed numerous vacation houses. There was more than sparse traffic now.

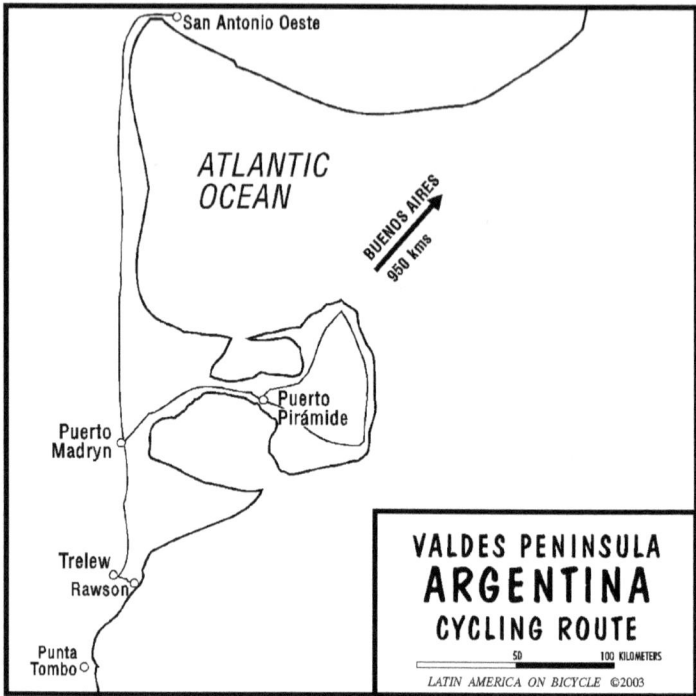

San Carlos de Bariloche is a tasteful, modern town with a Swiss look—high-peaked roofs, wooden shutters and siding, gables, porches. The streets go up and down the hillsides. We arrived tired, very, very tired, despite our boat rides. It might have been a good idea to have stayed the night in Llao Llao, where there were accommodations. But there were dozens of hotels to choose from in Bariloche, and as it was not yet January 1, we were in the low season. Our comfortable room cost about $5 per person.

Competition among restaurants on Mitre, the main street, was ferocious. German-style pastries, and of course wine and *bife*, were offered at the best prices we found in the country. There were no street money changers in this resort catering to Argentines, but shops specializing in imports eagerly took our dollars.

DAY ELEVEN

We spent two nights and a day in Bariloche, recouping and acting like tourists. Boats run from Llao Llao to Victoria Island, where there is a forestry research station; and to Bosque de los Arrayanes, a primeval myrtle forest where trees grow a centimeter a year, at the end of an arm of the lake. Walt Disney made a film there, we were told. The forest is eerie—trees are huge, intertwining, denuded of bark. Views of the cordillera from the island and lake are exceptional.

Back from the boat trip by early afternoon, I extracted my bicycle from the hotel and took a jaunt up to the ski center of Cerro Catedral. There were no less than thirty buses parked, early in summer, bringing teenagers to ride the cable cars. It looked great for skiing. As elsewhere in Argentina, my bike aroused curiosity, and people stopped to chat. Their French came in handy.

DAY TWELVE

We took advantage of the restaurants in Bariloche for lunch before leaving. It was an all-you-can-eat buffet, including a large piece of steak, soup, milk and dessert, all for less than $3. A biker's dream.

We had had a good experience with the train in Chile, and innocently we looked forward to our run across Argentina to San Antonio Oeste, on the Atlantic. We left at 1 p.m.

The train has ordinary class, with five-in-a-row seating, second class (in which we rode), and first class, which comes with air conditioning. The problem is that within ten minutes of leaving Bariloche, you are in the desert, the great Patagonian desert. Everything changes, from green alpine to dry. The few settlements are impoverished clusters of adobe houses amid the dust. And the dust isn't just in the landscape. It penetrates into the cars, you can't see anything for hours, it accumulates in layers several centimeters thick on the floor. Attendants sweep the dust back into the air. You cannot breathe. And after this, you arrive in the dead of night in San Antonio Oeste, a city with nothing of interest, nothing at all, where we stayed in the Vasquito, the town's minimal and only hotel.

DAY THIRTEEN

We ate well in a restaurant on the beach and took a bus for Puerto Madryn, about 200 kilometers to the south. They didn't want to take our bikes, but finally gave in. The two-and-a-half-hour ride was through perfectly flat, barren terrain.

But Puerto Madryn is an oasis, a well-built, pleasant resort town. We spent over an hour looking at hotels—that's one thing you can do easily on bicycle—and stayed at the Hotel Gran Madryn, on Calle Lugones. The cost was less than $15. There were many others to choose from, and a good camping site. It was December 31, and there were parties at many of the hotels.

DAY FOURTEEN

We weren't here only to test the resort qualities. Puerto Madryn is near the Valdés Peninsula, where several unusual ecosystems have survived and evolved apart from mainland wildlife. We wanted to go around the peninsula on bicycle.

We left Puerto Madryn about 10 a.m., having stocked up for the day. We should have left perhaps two hours earlier. Usually there is a mild breeze blowing seaward, but on this day, as we headed northeast to Puerto Pirámide, we cycled into a strong head wind. We fought on over the isthmus to the peninsula. Our water supply was insufficient for the battle. We should have had two and a half liters per person. The sun, the heat and the wind were all evaporating.

Isla de los Pájaros, just off the peninsula, is a reserve for sea birds, which nest in a shrub found on the island. The reserve is free not only of humans, who must content themselves with views from a distance through binoculars, but animal predators as well.

Past the bird reserve, onto the peninsula proper, the road took a turn to the southeast, and the wind began to hit us from the side. The going was easier. The peninsula, all of it a protected area, is bordered by cliffs. In the interior are salt flats, below sea level. The island is full of rheas, an ostrich-like bird, and guanacos, a relative of the llama.

As we approached Puerto Pirámide in the evening, we looked back, toward the Patagonian desert, to the greatest thunderstorm I had ever seen. We were exhausted. It was not that our road had been long—only 100 kilometers—but that we had gone up against the wind. We hoped to have the wind at our back when we retraced this route.

We checked into a clean hotel run by the Automóvil Club Argentino, one of several lodging places. The charge was $20 double. Despite the sea at the door, the menu was beef.

DAY FIFTEEN

I cycled out to the *Lobería*, about five kilometers from Puerto Pirámide, to see a colony of seals (*lobos marinos*, or sea wolves, in Spanish) on a beach at the base of a cliff, one of the few accessible places to view these creatures in the wild.

And then we put our bikes away for the day. It would have been possible to make a 225-kilometer circuit of the peninsula over gravel roads on a mountain bike, but we were going nowhere on our skinny tires. We tried to hitchhike, unsuccessfully, and ended up getting together with some other travellers to hire a car and driver to take us to Punta Norte. There, we looked at the only sea elephant colony on the continent. We saw more sea elephants along the beaches as we took a turn along the coast and continued south to Puerto Valdés. And there were penguins, penguins, penguins, coming up from their burrows, often in couples, waddling about and wading into the water and zooming off.

Offshore were the killer whales. One gobbled up a penguin, and strands of blood twirled in the water. Guanacos grazed everywhere. Another 150 kilometers south of Puerto Madryn, at Punta Tombo, is a concentration of a million penguins, notorious for its smell. We didn't get down that way.

DAY SIXTEEN

From Puerto Pirámide, we rode back to Puerto Madryn in four hours, then 50 kilometers south to Trelew, in another four hours. Trelew, and nearby Rawson, were settled by Welshmen, hence the non-Hispanic names, and also the Non-Hispanic Welsh faces out of which came Spanish sounds. Very strange, as had been the Spanish spoken by the Herren und Damen of Bariloche.

We stayed at the Touring Club's hotel in Trelew, the best for the price. The town is benign, small, of little interest but for the mini-botanical garden of the main square, with its huge trees and flowers in bloom.

Temperatures were reaching record highs of 40 Centigrade (104 Fahrenheit), too hot for cycling. At the beach, the water was too cold for swimming. We did not want to push our luck. The next day, took a plane to Buenos Aires.

One last bit of convenience was the luggage rack atop all taxis in Buenos Aires. We could easily put both our bikes on top, and secure them with elastic straps. We stayed at the Hotel San Antonio, at Calle Paraguay 372, for $21. There are many other reasonably priced hotels in the city.

Traffic was heavy and we put our bikes away in favor of our legs. Several of the streets are pedestrian malls, the most lively and elegant being Florida. The South American Handbook will guide you around the sights of the city, but one of the spots we passed which is not on the tourist map was the Escuela Mecánica, the torture chamber of the ex-military government, pointed out to us by our taxi driver.

If I go back again to Argentina, it will be with a mountain bike. I will try the northern route into the Andes from Mendoza, over the unpaved road. In Villavicencio, I will stay at a famous old-fashioned hotel, and test the thermal springs. Of course, I will call ahead to reserve, and I will leave Mendoza in the morning. And then there are the small towns around Mendoza, and the wineries. And the volcanoes in the south of Chile. And the ski resorts. And I will make sure that whoever I travel with is careful about the seafood.

9
COSTA RICA

No soldiers patrol the streets. Police are hard to find. Noisy demonstrations are held during free election campaigns. People appear to be healthy and reasonably well educated. Things work.

What a surprise! So many of the things we take for granted about North America and Western Europe apply to little Costa Rica as well, right in the middle of the turmoil and injustice and poverty of Central America.

The un-Latin American aspects of Costa Rica, and the rugged mountains, have led some to call it the Switzerland of Latin America. Sharp divisions in the population are not evident. There is little extreme poverty, and wealth is rarely ostentatious. Even the color of the people seems to be mostly the same light brown, though there are pockets of people of African and Indian heritage. The population is about 2,300,000, and the country appears to have ample resources to support them. Thirty percent of the national budget goes to education, which is free, there is a comprehensive social-security and medical-care system, and, most impressive, average life expectancy is over seventy years.

There have been major finds of pre-Columbian artifacts in Costa Rica, though there are no massive ancient cities to visit. Quaint oxcarts and picturesque local crafts are of interest to the visitor, as well as the general level of prosperity, education and effective public administration in a region not noted for these. But the main attractions in Costa Rica are its natural wonders. Active volcanoes overlook the capital. Vegetation ranges from the familiar to the exotic. An extensive system of national parks and protected areas takes in well over ten percent of the country's area, sheltering rare animals such as giant sea turtles, and unique plants and flowers, while affording visitors a chance to view these treasures. If there are other places in the Americas where you can practically shake hands with an ape in the open, or cycle up to inspect a fuming volcano crater, I don't yet know of them.

Costa Rica lies between the Caribbean and Pacific. A chain of mountains and volcanoes runs from northwest to southeast down its center. The climate ranges from sweltering to near-freezing, according to altitude. Most of the population lives in the Central Valley that includes the capital city, San José. There, at an altitude of about 1000 meters, the temperature is generally spring-like throughout the year. The dry time of the year in this area is from October to March, though there are occasional showers even in that period. The hot Pacific lowlands have a surer dry season, while along the Caribbean, coastal rains can blow in throughout the year as well.

Biking in Costa Rica is relatively safe. An extensive network of roads criss-crosses the central valley, and with few exceptions, there is no dense traffic. Almost all of these roads are paved. Outside of the central valley, there are fewer roads, but the density of population is quite low, so once again, traffic is light. The Pan American Highway, which links San José with Nicaragua and Panama, is well maintained. In some of the outlying areas in which we travelled, roads were unpaved, and in some stretches were rough going. But in general, the roads are good enough that you can see a large part of Costa Rica in a short amount of time by bicycle. It's nice to find all this "infrastructure" in a country that is not overly visited.

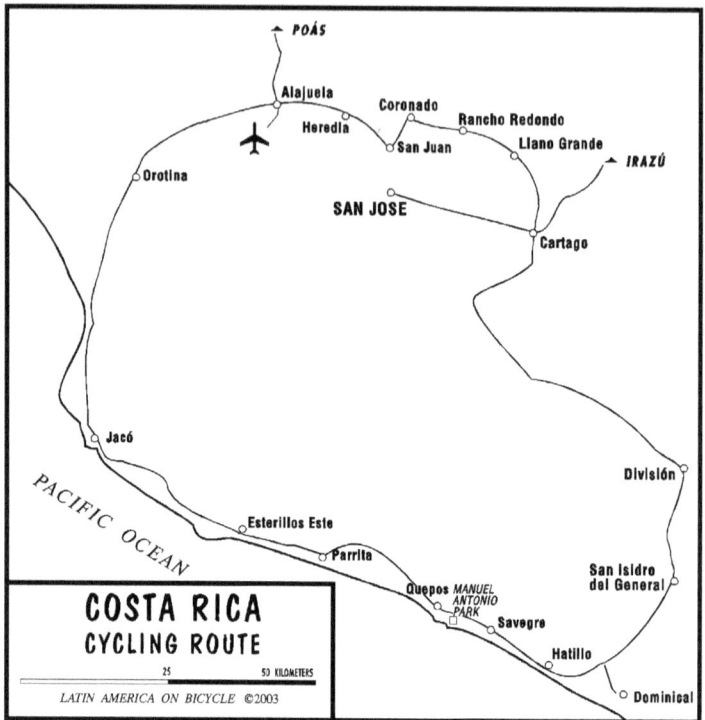

COSTA RICA
CYCLING ROUTE

LATIN AMERICA ON BICYCLE ©2003

The central valley, with its moderate grades, requires no special ability. Distances between towns are short. However, the up-and-down slopes along the edges of the valley, and ascents of the volcanoes, require good physical condition. Grades can be as great as ten percent, which is tough even for walking. At 2000 meters, the temperature is cool, and by 3000 meters—near the summit of volcanoes—it's cold. It also gets rainier the higher up you go. Stick to the lower altitudes if you absolutely can't deal with rain.

Travel through the flat Pacific lowlands was not overly strenuous, except in those stretches where the roads were unpaved. Even my companion, who usually suffers in the heat, did not find the temperature unbearable. In general, Costa Rica was good for a relatively laid-back style of cycling, with plenty of opportunity for admiring the landscape.

People in Costa Rica are friendly and kind. A couple of times we were stuck between towns, and were invited in for coffee or a meal. Our encounters were pleasant.

The official map of Costa Rica, published by the Geographical Institute of Costa Rica, is essential for the cyclist. No other map of comparable detail is available. The scale is 1:500,000, with a section showing the central region at 1:250,000. You can buy the map in San José at Librería Lehmann or Librería Universal, two large bookstores on Avenida Central. Every road is shown. The map published by the tourist office is useful for general orientation only, and for its street map of San José.

There are basic bicycle mechanic shops in most towns, in case you need an emergency repair to get you back on the road. We saw bicycles everywhere in Costa Rica, even on the worst roads.

I had a regular touring bike with eighteen speeds. I think twelve speeds are the minimum in terrain with as many grades as there are in Costa Rica. My companion had a mountain bike, which served her well on gravel roads and was in general a better bike for the conditions. But I had no problems and enjoyed the trip on my own bike.

We took buses on two occasions, and encountered only minor difficulties in doing so. Once we had to backtrack to the beginning of the line; the other time, several buses passed until we could get our bikes aboard.

We flew to San José on one airline, changing planes several times, following my personal strategy of entrusting our bicycles to one company. Our routing from Montreal required numerous stops along the way. The Costa Rican airline, LACSA, offers excursion fares from Miami, New Orleans and Los Angeles. And more and more, you can find charter flights in the busy season, when it's cold up north.

Most hotels in Costa Rica are clean, and the price is right for what they provide. We were generally satisfied. But there are some notable exceptions—and I do mean exceptions. We found out early on that when we arrived in a small town, we had to visit all hotels before deciding where we would stay. Some of the best hotels we stayed at were along the unpaved roads in the Pacific lowlands.

The price level in general in Costa Rica for food and lodging was at least 30 percent lower than what I'm used to at home. Bus fares and many other services cost much less. Food was generally simple but good and healthy. We ate heartily, and suffered no ill effects. If we had taken ill, I think that we would have been well taken care of. My companion, who is a doctor, had the general impression that medical services and health conditions in Costa Rica are quite good. There are, in fact, a number of world-class medical specialists who practice in San José.

DAY ONE

We left Montreal early, and by the time we reached Juan Santamaría airport, it was almost 9 p.m. local time. We got off to a bad start. Mechanical problems had forced a last-minute change of planes in New York, and our luggage had failed to follow.

Immigration and customs formalities were, well, informal, taking no more than a couple of minutes. No police, no soldiers, no hucksters interrupted our passage. Nor was there any tourist information, for that matter. The tourist office was closed, and it was closed when we came back the next day, and in fact it was closed when we were leaving the country as well.

The airport is just a few kilometers from Alajuela, one of the large towns of the Central Valley, and 17 kilometers from San José. As we would have to come back for our bikes, we decided to stay in Alajuela, a short bus ride away.

The simple but clean and bustling Hotel Alajuela was nearly full at the holiday season. As there are no other decent hotels in the town, a reservation would have been advisable. The rooms on the first floor, which open only onto the interior courtyard, are best, since they're sheltered from the early-morning noise of buses and cars leaving for San José. We paid $12 for a double room. A visitor looking for more amenities in a hotel, however, could find them at several hotels closer to the airport, or on the way to the capital.

One of the interesting—and disturbing—things we noted about the hotel was the shower in our bathroom, of a type we were to see all over the country. Live electrical wires came out of the wall and ran to a little appliance on the shower head that sizzled and smoked and instantly heated the water—somewhat. Let me tell you, as a trained electrical engineer, never to touch one of these devices, whether the water is running or not. I would be surprised if a certain number of people are not sizzled and smoked every year.

Alajuela is quite different, we were to find out, from the capital. Though near San José, it's not really a suburb. It is quiet, has a few good restaurants, and made a good low-key starting point.

DAY TWO

With all day to wait for the flight that would bring our bicycles, we decided to take a bus to the top of the Poás volcano. But first things first. We had to change money, a simple operation, as there was a bank near our hotel, on the main square.

Or so we thought. There was no lineup. Hardly any clients came in after us. And still it took an hour and a half to change our travellers checks, in a flurry of behind-the-counter activities the meaning of which I never did comprehend. Clearly, money exchange was something the traveller should not tackle very often in Costa Rica.

Nights in the Central Valley are cool, but it was soon warm as we looked for our bus. An orchestra played classical music in the main square, which was really an orderly little highland tropical forest, where sloths climbed among the treetops. The direct bus had already departed, but we found a bus to San Pedro, partway up the slopes. From San Pedro, a little agricultural town, we tried to hitchhike the rest of the way, but as you might imagine, there isn't much traffic headed to a dead end at the top of a volcano.

We ended up taking a taxi. For $20, we rode to the top of Poás, where the driver waited for more than an hour while we poked around.

It had been sunny down in the valley, but atop the volcano, at 2700 meters, clouds were shifting in and out, obscuring the sights for most of the time we were there. We were interested in getting a closer look at the steaming, water-filled main crater, until someone told me that a few years ago, some tourists went in and never came back.

Visitors are no longer allowed past the rim, but what we saw from that vantage point was impressive, despite the mist. The crater is huge, about a kilometer and a half across, one of the largest in the world. On the outskirts of the area made barren by hot volcanic steams and gases, vegetation is lush, with extremely large leaves, nourished by abundant moisture and volcanic ash. A modern visitors' center contains exhibits about volcanic activity and shows films about all of Costa Rica's national parks, of which Poás is a sort of flagship.

Back in Alajuela, we had dinner at the Cencerro restaurant. For about $6, we dined on steaks, at a table on a balcony overlooking the main square. Service was excellent, and all that was missing was a good wine—decent imported brands are prohibitively expensive. Not every restaurant we ate at in Costa Rica was as formal as the Cencerro, but in all cases the food was palatable. Frijoles—beans—were an inevitable mealtime fixture.

In the evening, we took a bus to the airport, where our luggage arrived with the next flight. We assembled our bikes, and it took us just a few minutes to cycle back to our hotel, on a well-marked road. All the roads in Costa Rica, we found, are well posted, not only with route numbers, but with directional signs for towns at every junction.

So that was the first full day of our bicycle trip in Costa Rica, mostly without wheels of our own. Which turned out just as well, for I doubt that we would otherwise have left ourselves time to see Poás volcano.

DAY THREE

We left Alajuela, following a road toward San José that parallels the main superhighway, and soon found ourselves in a bicycle race. Crowds lined both sides of the road, a helicopter hovered above, television and film cameras recorded the goings-on, fans cheered for their favored participants, and for us as well. We were offered water, which we didn't need, but which we accepted graciously.

With our baggage, we made lousy racers. Before long, the real racers caught up and overtook us and disappeared into the distance, leaving us once again to acknowledge the kind wishes of the crowds. There were participants from a number of countries, but beyond that, I do not know the name or significance of the race. It was a stroke of luck, however, as motor vehicles were barred from the route. The road was fairly flat all the way, and, beyond the fans, lined with small factories of one sort or another. Coffee plantations stretched off into the distance.

At Heredia, we left the path of the race, which seemed to be heading toward San José. Our plan was to skirt the capital, which we would be visiting at the end of the trip. Our route would be through small towns to the north, toward the Irazú volcano, on the slopes of which was a good hotel, according to our guidebook.

We cycled through Santo Domingo to San Juan, both clean towns with light industry, then took a wrong turn, onto a highway that was under construction. By the time we realized what we had done, we were several kilometers on the way toward the rainy eastern lowlands, which we had no intention of getting to know on this trip. Too bad. The road was newly paved, and in excellent condition.

We returned to our intended route by a side road, through one of the few areas where we saw very poor people. I don't mean that they were destitute, in the way of dwellers in cardboard slums, but their wooden houses clung to the mud on both sides of a canyon.

Here, on the wrinkles of land above San José, we were going up and down continually, on mild grades. It was cool, and as it was our first day on the road and we were not yet into our routines, we neglected to apply enough sunscreen. We paid for our lack of caution with sunburn.

We pedalled through sleepy San Vicente, and up into San Isidro de Coronado, a hill town and farming center with fine views down to the capital in the distance. Here we were surprised to find a huge Gothic church that seemed rather out of context. Between the church towering over the country town, and the temperate-zone vegetation, I had the feeling of passing through rural Quebec. We noted a few rather substantial houses. But most of the homes were simple and well-maintained, and almost all had a family coffee grove.

Beyond Coronado, the road was as good as you could want it for cycling, well-surfaced, with little traffic, and mountain and valley views to either side. We went up, up, and up again. The views to the volcanoes, and to San José below, were magnificent. But as we pedalled, we began to realize that we had done some poor planning. It was getting late in the day, certainly for this place and time of year, where night fell at 6 p.m. We had left Alajuela at noon, after a visit to the bank once again, leaving ourselves limited daylight travel time, with a long road ahead of us, and little information about conditions and facilities along the way.

We arrived at Rancho Redondo, about 700 meters above San Isidro, well after dark, and found that the road beyond was unpaved. With no accommodations in sight, we continued on gravel, using our flashlights for illumination, still ascending, though less markedly. It took two and a half hours to get over the dirt and rocks and climb another 200 meters to Llano Grande, walking a good part of the way, pushing our bicycles with one hand, flashlight in the other.

We were tired and hungry, and must have looked it, for a family took pity on us and invited us to share their simple meal of a stew of potatoes with bits of meat. Potatoes were grown all around us on the lower slopes of Irazú, on land enriched by fallout from eruptions that intermittently made this area notably unsafe. There were four children in the family that hosted us. The oldest slept in a bed built into the wall, and closed off with planks. It looked like a tomb. The mother appeared to be in her forties but was probably younger. Her husband had died three years before, and she was still quite affected. She showed us his photo. We could have stayed with this family if we had had sleeping bags. But as we were not so equipped and it was very cold—even at 9 p.m.—we continued on our way in the dark.

Through the cold, cloudless sky, we could see the light of an antenna that stands atop Irazú, and the glow shining up from the valley below. But the scenery all around us, which we had wanted to savor, remained unrevealed. We followed a paved road down from Llano Grande, toward the carpet of lights of Cartago and surrounding villages. We arrived at 11 p.m., after getting final directions from some monks outside a monastery.

There were no decent accommodations in Cartago, but we did not want to go to San José by bus, if, indeed, any operated at that hour. Our lodging place was the Hotel Familial, the name of the establishment deriving, I have no doubt, from the families of cockroaches that dwell therein. The manager was drunk, and we thought we had walked into Beirut, to judge by the jagged holes in the walls. We brought our bicycles into the room, and slept in our clothes, sort of. In the morning I took a shower in a stall that had probably been used for other purposes.

I say with hindsight that we should have left Alajuela at 7 a.m. We could then have continued in daylight past Llano Grande to Tierra Blanca, and onto the road up the Irazú volcano. This would have spared us dropping down into Cartago, from which we had to ascend again the next day. The hotel on the volcano's slopes is two hours on bicycle from Tierra Blanca, which means a full, long day from Alajuela. Of course, one could simply stay in San José, but we preferred our meandering route through small towns, that varied from industrialized near San José to more rural and slow-paced the farther out we went.

DAY FOUR

The market of Cartago is near the railway station, the ambience of which brought us back to 1920 or so, with its old, tin-roofed structure, and the hustle and bustle of carts in the streets all around. We bought some food to replenish our stocks.

And then we started up toward the Hotel Montaña Irazú. And I do mean up. Cartago is at an altitude of about 1000 meters. Twenty kilometers away by road is the summit of Irazú, at about 3500 meters. Which makes a grade of over ten percent. That's on the average. Obviously, in some parts it was going to be greater. I had never tackled such a long, tilting climb.

The road was in very good condition, paved all the way to the top. Traffic was moderate for about five kilometers out of Cartago, after which it was quite light. But the route was relentless. A few trucks passed, and perhaps the drivers could have been prevailed upon by the weary for a lift.

Along the way on the slopes of Irazú, at Tierra Blanca, at about 2000 meters, is a cluster of stores where you can buy soft drinks. We had learned by this time that Canada Dry was the brand to ask for. Canada Dry ginger ale is available everywhere in Costa Rica.

We continued upward past cattle pastures, and fields planted in potatoes. Four kilometers past the Tierra Blanca junction, we stopped at a roadside viewpoint. Children were selling cucumbers marinated in brine, no doubt a local cottage-industry specialty. They looked good, but the road did not encourage us to take on the added weight.

For several kilometers on both sides, the road was lined with eucalyptus trees, and as we pedalled and sweated, we savored their delicious aroma.

We arrived at the Hotel Montaña Irazú at about 3 p.m., having left Cartago at 10 a.m., and checked in and called it a day. It was sunny and warm. The hotel was a large, green, colonial-style building, with a restaurant on the first floor and all the guest rooms upstairs. One large family appeared to be in charge of the restaurant, the mother and kids running the kitchen, serving guests, and sleeping there as well.

The sun went down, and suddenly, it was very, very cold. The rooms were not heated, except for the shower, and its output was temperamental. Once again, we wished we had brought sleeping bags. The damp and chilling air penetrated through our ten—yes, ten—covers. We felt a little bit disoriented, having left Canada for warm climes, and finding ourselves on the first of January huddled around the fireplace in the dining room, tipping one of the kids to throw on more wood, as the wind whistled outside. At least it didn't snow.

We spent two nights at the Montaña Irazú, which was, aside from the evening chill, in all respects pleasant. It is rustic, built largely of wood, which allows the night chill and wind inside. A village is located nearby, and the inhabitants come to the hotel to pass their evenings, drinking in the bar, chatting, and playing cards. The electricity was cut off at night, and we had to rely on our flashlights when we weren't stargazing through the clear mountain air.

Our clean, adequate room cost about $10 double. Meals were hearty—breakfast of eggs and beans, and steaks for dinner, served with fried plantains and fresh local vegetables—good for bikers, with no risk of illness at that altitude. The witching hour at the hotel was 9 p.m. The bar emptied out, doors were locked for the night, the staff disappeared, and if you arrived looking for a room you would be out of luck.

DAY FIVE

We took a day trip to the top of Irazú. When we left in the morning it was sunny. The distance to the summit was only seven kilometers, but of course these were the steepest kilometers I was to encounter. Two kilometers past our hotel was a restaurant that catered to day visitors. It claims to be the highest restaurant in Central America, which I think must be true. We stopped there for a meal later, on our descent. The food was as good as at our hotel, and there was a magnificent mountain and valley view. We had gallo pinto, chicken with rice and beans and assorted other items thrown in, which is served throughout the country. There was one oddity: the walls were decorated with thousands of business cards left by visitors. The restaurant appeared to be a favorite stopping point for people making day outings from San José.

Near the summit of the volcano, the vegetation changed markedly, from open fields and pastures to small, weatherbeaten little fir trees. We were closed in by fog, and couldn't see more than a few meters ahead as we pedaled the last stretch.

The top of Irazú is flat, and what did we find but a soccer match in progress. A sign indicated dates of major eruptions, which had been at intervals of fifteen to twenty years. We were more than a little bit concerned—the last major blowup had been in 1966. We didn't stay long.

The clouds cleared for a while. We couldn't see both oceans, which is said to be possible at times, but the view was extensive, both of the two craters of the volcano itself and of the countryside spreading out below.

I had not experienced much difficulty in slowly pedalling up, but strangely, once I dismounted and started to walk around, I felt the effect of the altitude. While not exerting myself, I huffed and puffed and panted for more and more thin air.

A kiosk sold postcards, and also sodas, but otherwise, Irazú was quite different from the well-outfitted peak of Poás. There were no facilities for visitors other than a few signs, and we truly felt that we had arrived at one of the ends of the world. The main crater was full of water dark and dirty with minerals and assorted volcanic ejecta, and the surrounding area was pitted, bare of all but the most tenuous vegetation, positively lunar in aspect.

We descended back down the road on our brakes, as a driving rainstorm rolled in. After lunch, we took it easy at our hotel. The rain finally ceased at night, driven off by a howling wind.

DAY SIX

Returning is not the same as going, especially down a volcano. We rolled to Cartago in an hour and a half, a ride without event, except that it was raining, raining, raining. About five kilometers out of Cartago, as we left Irazú's slopes, the rain ceased. But with rain gear, gloves and woolen hats, we had not been put out, and our reflective vests made us visible to the few buses and cars that passed us. As we descended, we sensed the air warming up, becoming richer.

Cartago is noticeably poorer than San Jose. We looked around, especially at the basilica for which the town is known. But there is not much to interest a visitor.

Our plan for the day was to take a bus to San Isidro de El General, to the southeast. At 800 meters, San Isidro is lower than the Central Valley towns. Our information indicated that there was only one poor hotel along the way, and after our experience of the Hotel Familial, we did not want to risk having to stay in it. Also, to reach San Isidro on bicycle, we would have to follow the Pan American Highway over Cerro de la Muerte—Peak of Death—the highest point on the road in Central America. We would probably run into rain in the mountains, even at this time of the year, and not see much.

We tried to stop a bus for San Isidro on the Pan American Highway outside of Cartago, but in vain. People were making holiday trips, and all the buses were full. What we had to do in the end was take a taxi to San José, where the buses started out. This cost us a few hours. Our tickets were $5 each, with another $2 charged for our bikes. These had to go in a second bus, which we were told would follow us, and indeed it did, though I had some misgivings, and I'm not sure I would have accepted such an arrangement in another country.

Along the way, the driver stopped every now and then, in the middle of nowhere, to allow kids to climb aboard and peddle snacks—fried plantains, tortillas and pastries with fillings—no doubt prepared that morning in mom's kitchen. For their cooperation, the drivers had free eats.

Not much was visible from the bus in the mist and fog, but we did note an area of paramo, the strange, specialized vegetation of harsh tropical altitudes that occurs only in Colombia, Venezuela, Ecuador and Costa Rica. Many of the characteristic plants are windblown and dwarflike, but there is also an eerie species of dandelion that grows up to five feet in height. This was probably the northernmost area of such growth.

We stayed on the bus all the way to San Isidro, but in retrospect, a better plan would have been to get off at La Ese, about ten kilometers before, or División, twenty kilometers out, in order to appreciate the landscape better. Besides, plummeting down a mountain road in a Latin American bus is always unnerving for me. I figure it would be an easy two-hour descent from División to San Isidro.

In the Central Valley, we had hardly felt ourselves to be in Central America, but at San Isidro, we were in the tropics. The climate is relatively warm, and sheltered from rain in January, though slightly humid. The slopes in the region were planted to coffee, but the streets of the town were lined by majestic palms. The white church stands out in that green sea. Towering above is the Talamanca mountain range, covered with dark clouds. But the clouds stayed at the distant peaks, and it never rained on us in San Isidro.

We arrived after four, and could have stayed at any of several modest hotels in town. But we had learned of a good hotel, the Del Sur, six kilometers out on the road to Panama. The hotel is managed by a cooperative—the cooperative movement is quite strong in Costa Rica, and we saw double-pine-tree symbols everywhere. It also serves as a training school for hotel personnel. It was modern and very clean, and we stayed a couple of days, enjoying the pool and excellent service.

DAY SEVEN

We spent some time wandering around San Isidro, which is the major city of the southeast. One restaurant, on the west side of the central park, served us an especially good stew, and yuca, a tasty tropical root vegetable. The Dos Pinos dairy cooperative operates a store in town, where we enjoyed ice cream—something we would generally not do in the tropics, where milk products are suspect. Most of the people we saw seemed to be agricultural workers.

There are no great touristic landmarks in San Isidro, but there are dozens of the lesser attractions and oddities of a quiet provincial center. Near the main square, a huge Norfolk pine tree in a rock garden was decorated for Christmas. Members of a local Hare Krishna community looked out of place. A dental surgeon advertised painless extraction on his nameplate. Then there were several children who passed by with plaster casts. My companion, who specializes in orthopedic surgery, stopped and stared. The casts could not have been for broken arms, broken fingers, broken anything. They had been applied in places that served no purpose.

Several excursions were available to us. One would have been to Chirripó National Park, which includes extensive areas of protected paramo vegetation. Another one suggested to us was up the valley of the Chirripó River, on the road toward Rivas, climbing into the Talamanca range. Our time, however, was limited, and I would have needed a mountain bike.

DAY EIGHT

We left San Isidro and headed south, toward Dominical and the coast. The road is paved only for a couple of kilometers, after which its condition ranges from average to poor to quite poor. The general slope of the road is down, but we had to descend into and climb out of the valley of the Pacuare River, and cross a mountain spur. Several times we had to walk. The road is lined with large coffee plantations, which have their own private roads and bridges and processing centers, and are active little universes in themselves.

At one point, about 25 kilometers out of San Isidro, we encountered a man who was just walking along, at some distance from any settlement. His Spanish was poor, he carried no baggage, he looked as if he survived along the roads as well as he could. We gave him some food, which he gobbled down right in front of us. You don't find this kind of vagabond very often in Costa Rica.

Once we descended to the coastal plain, the condition of the road was better. Though it was still of earth, in the dry season it was hard and flat. Large birds hovered overhead, like the vultures that indicate impending death in films. The change in vegetation was drastic. We were really in a jungle. It was hot and sunny.

At Barú, we took the poor branch road to Dominical, a beach resort, where we found that most of the hotels were full. We followed a new gravel road five kilometers onward to Punta Dominical, where we had been told there was another hotel, run by Americans. The Hotel-Cabinas Punta Dominical was a find, a collection of clean and comfortable bungalows, set on a cliff above a rocky beach. Our room had sea views, and we could hear the waves gently rolling ashore all night. The cost was $20 double. This compared to a $15 rate at some filthy beachfront shacks in Dominical itself. We dined at the simple bar on giant river shrimp, for a few dollars each.

DAY NINE

At dawn we left for Puerto Quepos. At one point, as I trailed behind my companion, I saw an iguana cross onto the road. She and the iguana were unaware of each other as they headed in the same direction. When the iguana was a couple of feet from her bicycle, the two travellers suddenly noticed each other. The iguana jumped several feet in the air, and my friend nearly did the same. When both regained their equilibrium, they headed in opposite directions. It was a big iguana, one that could have knocked over the bicycle had the encounter been closer.

In Dominical, we chanced upon a soccer game, which, I guess, was a regular Sunday morning activity, despite the heat. All of the participants were dressed in shorts and drenched in sweat.

We had to backtrack to Barú to cross a river and continue up the coast—a new bridge was under construction right at Dominical. The road was quite poor. Near Hatillo, we saw oranges piled atop a table at a roadside stand, next to a sign reading "J.-G. Urbain." Nobody was in attendance. Parched, our thirst heightened by the sight of the fruit, we called out "yoo-hoo" to whoever was lurking in the jungle ready to serve customers. Nobody answered. But we wanted those oranges, and after five minutes, we called again. A female voice answered our cries with her own "yoo-hoo," but nobody appeared, so we "yoo-hooed" even louder, and after another five minutes, there appeared a man. He was clean-shaven, in his forties. We asked if we could buy oranges, and after about 30 seconds we mutually realized that we were both from Quebec. He turned out to be from Ahuntsic, in the northern part of Montreal. He told us that his wife visited once or twice a year, and that he lived pretty well on his own, cultivating cacao and other crops. He seemed to be accepted by the local people, whose voices we had heard from the jungle. We chatted for about an hour, but didn't find out what he was doing misplaced among the orange trees in a remote coastal tropical village. Perhaps there wasn't anything to find out. He seemed happy enough, I just wondered how he had ended up there.

Beyond Hatillo, the road continued inland from the ocean—not far inland, but enough that we couldn't see the water. Rice was cultivated on large farms, owned, according to Mr. Jean-Guy Urbain, by Americans. And land was expensive in these parts.

We crossed rivers and rivers and rivers on the way to Matapalo. This was in the dry season; I think it would have been quite difficult to do so after serious rains. The first streams I rode through. Others I waded. The rivers were wider and deeper the nearer we got to Matapalo. The water came up above the middle of my bicycle. Trucks and buses splashed right through. At one river, I had to carry my luggage across, then return for my bicycle. Luckily, the current was slow. We got wet, of course, but it was warm, so it wasn't too bad.

Some days later, farther up the coast, we crossed a river similar to these, on a bridge. We looked down and saw an alligator, and wondered about the innocent-appearing logs we had seen in streams earlier. Cattle waded in these waters in places, but I wouldn't recommend tarrying for a swim.

Near Matapalo, we crossed a steel bridge with pedestrians, while cars and trucks splashed through the water. On the other side was a little settlement of oval huts made of thatch—both walls and roof. Nowhere else did we see such basic, poor dwellings.

The country was nearly flat, with some gradual ascents and descents. It was getting to be a long day, even with only 50 kilometers or so to cover. You don't go very fast on a gravel road, probably at half or a third of your pace on a paved road. It was dry everywhere on the coast in this season, and we had to drink large quantities of Canada Dry. At Savegre we crossed over a large bridge, then followed the road farther inland, through a vast palm oil plantation. Perfectly straight rows of palms stretched away from us, and the road cut through them, also disciplined and straight as a runway. We encountered many people getting around from one part of the plantation to another on heavy bicycles. Identical wooden company houses were painted in assorted pastel colors to lend them individual distinction. Basic needs seemed, at a glance, to be well taken care of. But it was, nevertheless, dreary.

Past the Naranjo river, the landscape changes. Cliffs jutted up on the seaward side of the road. At a junction, we turned left, to follow the road into Quepos.

We arrived at Puerto Quepos at 6 p.m., as the sun was setting. The town is tumbledown, a tropical port. People are kind and the place is safe, but being of a seedy appearance, it doesn't look safe. There are several hotels, but Quepos is not a place in which visitors choose to stay.

We turned southeast, and continued onward and upward, over a ridge, toward Punta Quepos, seven kilometers away, and Manuel Antonio National Park. The road is paved, but the ascent in the first half is strenuous. At the highest point on the road is the Hotel Mariposa, which is elegant and expensive— over $100 for a double room. The Divisamar, across the road, was quite nice, clean and well-maintained, and moderately priced at $40 for a double. But they had no room. The helpful staff sent us down the road toward the Colibrí. This turned out to be a sort of a bed-and-breakfast establishment, run by Pierre and Gilles, a couple of Montrealers. The charge was only $10 per person. The views from the balcony to the sea below the cliff and the setting sun were good—maybe not up to those at the Mariposa, but the price was cut-rate. These two fellows cultivated orchids on their lot, and one worked at a French restaurant in Quepos, after preparing a large breakfast for his guests. Being above the beach, we had a climb when we went back to our room.

We ate at an American-run restaurant near the Divisamar. It looked overly touristy, but turned out to serve good food at a fair price. Another restaurant, German-run, near Quepos, served Italian cuisine. We ate an excellent vegetarian lasagne there.

I also can't fail to mention here as well the best pineapples I have ever had. These are sold at the entrance to Manuel Antonio park—at least they were in season at the time of our visit. The deft vendors will cut them up for you, without touching them with their hands.

Then there was the dessert we had one evening at the dining room of the pricey Mariposa. I remember it, but it was not memorable. We were promised something exquisite, which turned out to be an ordinary dry piece of cake slathered with marshmallow spread from a jar. I suspect the spread was imported, and we were expected to appreciate it.

DAY TEN

I had never seen apes outside the zoo, until I looked up into the trees behind the Colibrí, and spotted several swinging in the branches.

We walked down from the Colibrí to Punta Quepos, and the beaches of Manuel Antonio park. There are several other hotels and lodging places at the base of the cliff, and along the beaches, but in general, they are not as nice as those above.

The three beaches here range from fully sheltered and calm, to one with large waves. Take your choice. A small museum orients visitors to the animal and plant life. Offshore are coral reefs. Masks and fins can be rented at some of the hotels. The vines and air plants and huge trees of the rain forest come down almost to the water's edge.

I was hesitant to go too far into the jungle, being afraid of snakes and tigers and other creatures that lurked in fact or in my imagination. But once I ventured onto the Punta Catedral trail, I was well rewarded. Toucans and macaws and birds of all colors that I had only dreamed of sat on branches and darted about. Groups of apes, black and white, came quite close. One looked me straight in the eyes. I looked back, saw an intelligent, near-human face, and nearly engaged him in conversation. Sloths oozed along. The trail can be walked in a hurry in fifteen minutes, but is worth an hour or two.

DAY THIRTEEN

After two idyllic days around Manuel Antonio we were on the road at 8 a.m. The paved road out of Puerto Quepos lasted seven kilometers or so. Soon we were passing through palm plantations again, and crossing numerous rivers, but on bridges. It was sunny, humid and warm, and we drank volumes of Canada Dry. We stopped and ate at a bar in Parrita, a dusty palm-oil town. Near Esterillos Este we noted numerous signs advertising the Hotel del Sol. We took a look, found it to be a clean place, but a bit of a ripoff, and as it was still early in the day, we continued toward Jacó.

The road took an inland direction, with green humps of mountains rising up to either side. A few kilometers before we reached the sea again, at Pochotal, the asphalt began. For me, with a touring bike, it was like coming out of an unsettling dream, and into a pleasant one. We picked up speed, cycled above and then along the ocean, and soon were in Jacó. We arrived at 4 p.m., having left Quepos at 8 a.m. and made numerous stops.

Jacó is a developed resort, with an airstrip. The waters are not crystalline, but are warm and pleasant enough, though at high tide currents are strong. We found the town to be of human proportions, pleasant for walking around. We shopped at the bakery, and tried the barbecued chicken at Pollo Asado Borinquen, run by Americans.

Our hotel was the clean, quiet, German-run Cocal, right along the sea, which charged about $15 per person, and had a swimming pool. We stayed there two nights, and had no complaints. Most groups go to the large Jacó Beach Hotel, where dance bands play into the night.

DAY FIFTEEN

We left early in the morning, as the day warms up quickly. But it was not early enough to avoid the heat.

The road turned inland, and past Patos, a few kilometers on, wound up and down hillsides. We could see the Nicoya Peninsula in the distance, across twenty kilometers of blue water, and farther down the Gulf of Nicoya, the city of Puntarenas jutting out into the sea. We reached the coast again at Tárcoles, then turned up toward San José, through hill country. Cattle ranches replaced the coastal plantations. The road was in good condition, with little traffic. But we were more exposed to the sun than we had been along the coast, where the breeze and the shade of trees had provided some relief. Now we ascended on naked south-facing slopes protected by hills from the wind—open-air ovens. We had some relief on shaded downhill stretches.

By 2 p.m. we were in Orotina, a rural trading center, where we noted a large Jehovah's Witnesses hospital.

From Orotina, it would have been an ascent all the way to San José on our bikes, along one of the busiest roads in the country. We considered taking the train, but decided on the faster bus service.

While we waited at the main square, I had an an ice cream that upset my stomach. We sat and watched town life under the large shade trees. People sold granizadas—the local snow cones—and coconuts, into which they chopped a hole for a straw. Townspeople sat and chatted and passed the time. Several buses came and went before we found one that would accept our bicycles.

By 6 p.m. we were in San José. We checked into the Hotel Gran Vía, where for $30 we had a room with a balcony overlooking the action on one of the capital's main thoroughfares. The show was better than on the t.v. in the room. A presidential election campaign was in progress, and demonstrations took place in the street below our window, and across the way in the Plaza de la Cultura, a city square decorated with modern sculpture and provided with an amphitheater.

DAY SIXTEEN

San José is a modest, moderately paced capital. We poked our way through more demonstrations, seeing the sights—an impressive national theater, an archeological museum in a Spanish fortress—and at 1 p.m. rode westward out of town on the old main highway. There were slums on the way, which were noticeable because there are relatively few of them in Costa Rica.

Taking secondary roads, we headed to Ojo de Agua, a large spring that fills several swimming pools and also supplies water for distant Puntarenas. We swam for about an hour, and continued to familiar Alajuela nearby. This was a convenient place to make our preparations for departure the next morning.

We spent the evening at the movies. I have never seen as many cinemas in a town of its size as I did in Alajuela. With a choice of half a dozen movies, we saw Amadeus, in English with Spanish subtitles. Tickets cost less than a dollar. But there was no popcorn. It was a pleasant, low-key last evening before our departure. I nearly fell asleep, but not because of the movie. I was tired.

I left after a good sampling of Costa Rica. But I didn't see all that I wanted to. On my next trip to Costa Rica, I will cycle down to the Caribbean, and take the famous jungle train back to the capital. And head out into some of the national parks, on a mountain bike.

10
GUATEMALA

A glance at a topographical map of Guatemala shows a country criss-crossed by mountain chains, volcanoes and rivers, sectored into numerous steep valleys. A trip through the country on bicycle could mean unlimited huffing and puffing, ascending steep grades at the pace of a snail in subtropical heat, lashed by seasonal rains, battered by coastal winds.

A bit more of a delve into the facts, however, reveals that some of the apparent disadvantages are just not there, while others could make for a truly memorable excursion.

In Guatemala, travel at a moderate pace is an advantage. In the course of a few hours on the pedals, the visitor can encounter a dozen Indian villages, each with its unique dialect and style of dress; cross from barren, frigid zones that see snow flurries on the coldest nights of the year to the languid heat of the tropics, and then back up to enchanted valleys that know nothing but springtime; travel from a metropolis of cars and computers to a world little changed from before the gasoline era, where human beings, not machines, till and irrigate crops, bear huge burdens on their backs, and turn out crude furniture and exquisite textiles as their forebears have for centuries.

All this passes by at a pace too quick for absorption when seen from a car or bus hurtling over the highways; but the

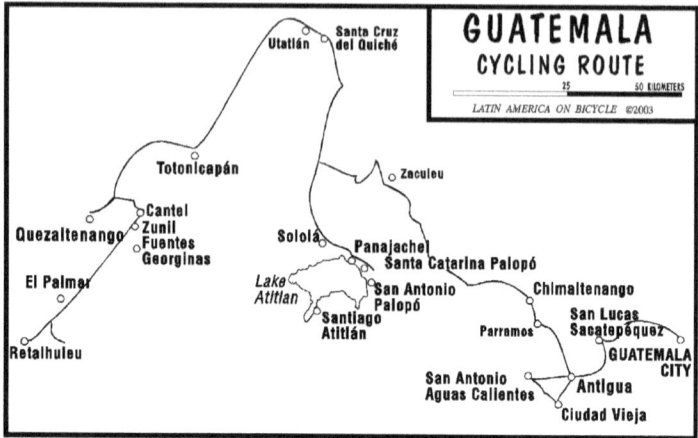

GUATEMALA
CYCLING ROUTE

LATIN AMERICA ON BICYCLE ©2003

pace of a bicycle is just about right. Access to unspoiled villages and magnificent scenery is far more easy than anywhere else I've been.

Like some other Central American countries, Guatemala is almost a continent in miniature. In a relatively small area are not only mountains, volcanoes and lakes, but also hot jungle lowland, savannah, and even near-desert. What sets Guatemala apart from its neighbors, however, is a fascinating and varied human geography, a rich colonial heritage, and the remains of advanced pre-Columbian civilizations.

Let me make it clear that a tour of Guatemala is within the capabilities of the average biker, despite the rugged terrain. On most days, we did not cover long stretches, because there was so much to stop and see. There are no marathon distances over desert or mountain, and the temperature in the highlands, where we spent most of our time, was generally comfortable. There was only one stretch that we travelled—the dirt road between Santa Cruz del Quiché and Totonicapán—that required more than average physical conditioning, but we could have taken an easier, longer route had we chosen.

There aren't a lot of trunk highways in Guatemala, but those that exist are in good condition. Secondary, unpaved roads are generally transitable—if your tires have generous rubber, and if you do not choose to travel at the height of the rainy season (May to October in most of the country). From Guatemala City, one major, heavily trafficked highway leads northeastward to the Caribbean; the other runs south toward the Pacific, then westward through the country's richest plantation land. But, fortunately for the cycle tourist, the most interesting parts of the country are elsewhere. My route took me and my companion for the most part through the western highlands, an area largely bypassed by modern export agriculture. Except near major towns, traffic is light.

Guatemala was the first country in Latin America that I toured on a mountain bike. Though most of our travel was on paved roads, I would not have done without wide tires and sturdy frame on stretches of gravelly, sandy, potholed and poorly graded secondary roads.

The climate in Guatemala is no problem. Most of the time I was comfortable in shorts and t-shirt. At night and in the early morning during the dry season it is not just cool, but cold in many places. At the beginning and end of the day I wore a sweater and light jacket, and at night I wore a tuque (woolen cap) as well.

Toward April, daytime and evening temperatures get warmer. If you absolutely have to travel during the rainy season, go in June, when there is some letup. My trip was in January, and I didn't see a drop of rain in the highlands.

Because Guatemala is densely populated in the most scenic and interesting areas, and cars are few, buses are everywhere! Where we did not consider a highway safe for cycling, where we did not want to retrace our route, and when we wanted to reach a town with acceptable accommodations by nightfall, we never had to wait more than a few minutes to flag down a bus going in our direction. Our bikes went on top, we went inside on the bench seats, and hardly any money left our pockets.

We saw numerous bicycle repair shops in Guatemala, where we probably could have had temporary repairs made. It was never hard to find a small store selling bottled sodas, canned juices, and cookies. Those basics which are available throughout the country are packaged in the small quantities that people can afford. It was a convenience to buy a ten-cent package of laundry detergent, and not have leftovers to leak in our luggage.

Airlines offer few discounts to Guatemala, Our ticket from Montreal to Guatemala City cost almost $600, and the fare can be even higher during busy periods. There are cheaper ways to go, using bargain fares to Miami or New Orleans, or by flying through Mexico to the Guatemalan border. I chose my usual through routing with a single carrier, however, to minimize interline handling of my bike.

In this case, the airline charged an additional $40 round trip to carry my bike.

A map of Guatemala can be obtained at no charge at the tourist information desk at the airport. For planning your day's ride, a variety of useful, detailed maps is available at low cost from the Instituto Geográfico Militar (Military Geographic Institute), Avenida Las Américas 5-76, Zone 13, not far from the Guatemala City airport.

We stayed in hotels ranging from quite good to rather basic, and rates for what we got were always surprisingly modest. We generally found the food to be safe, and only cooked for ourselves a couple of times.

The currency in Guatemala is the quetzal, which at the time of our visit had an official rate and a black-market rate. Banks will pay slightly less than the black-market rate, but it's safer to use their facilities than to hand money over to strangers on the street. Outside of Guatemala City, banks are sometimes scarce, so be sure to change enough money to cover your expenses for a few days before leaving the capital.

DAY ONE

We arrived at Aurora Airport, the location of which, on the southern outskirts of Guatemala City, is perfect for bicyclists. No hotel, even in the most distant old downtown area, is more than five kilometers from the terminal.

We were late getting in—a fire had delayed our departure by two hours—and all airport shops were closed. But the tourist information booth remained open, and the lady on duty was most helpful in finding a hotel for our budget and making sure there was a room available.

We assembled our bicycles in the luggage area. Immediately I noted an open flap on one of my bags. A waterproof flashlight had been filched from an outer pocket. I tried to make a report, but to no avail. All personnel had already gone home. The airline had let me down for a second time that day. I had counted on it providing me with a large cardboard box for my bike bags, as it had on a past trip. Without a box, I had taped all my bags shut, but this had not been enough. (I did manage to file a report and get compensation later, and in any case, my companion had a flashlight as well.)

With our bags tied on, we wheeled through customs and rode into town. We followed a divided boulevard out of the airport to Boulevard Liberación, shown on maps as Diagonal 12, turned right, and continued four blocks and around a traffic circle onto Avenida La Reforma, which passes by or near a number of hotels. When in doubt about where to turn, we simply motioned to drivers, who pulled over, answered our questions, and pointed the way. Everyone was friendly.

The city is divided into zones. Hotels in zones 9, 10 and 4 are closest both to the airport and to the highway leading out of town toward the western highlands. These are also relatively pleasant areas, from which the older, noisier, more polluted downtown (Zone 1, to the north) can be easily reached by bus. Traffic in the city appears to be moderate to heavy during the daytime, but it is possible to cycle safely. At night, the streets are very, very quiet.

We reached the Hotel Plaza and were settled in for the night within 30 minutes of leaving the airport. This hotel is in a noisy part of Zone 4. The rate for two for a plain room is about $20. We didn't intend to stay for long; virtually everything of interest in Guatemala is outside of the capital. A few blocks away, at Residencial Reforma, a block from the U.S. embassy, more elegant rooms in a converted mansion are about $25, a better value. When we were in Guatemala City again before leaving the country, we stayed at Guest House Alemana, at 4 Avenida and 14 Calle, Zone 10, in a very quiet neighborhood. The rate was $18 double, and we were pleased with the clean accommodations.

We found almost immediately upon arrival that the reaction of Guatemalans to us was low-key. This held throughout our trip. We could work on our bicycles and not be bothered by anybody. Guatemalans seemed extraordinarily tolerant.

We also noted on the streets a preponderance of personnel of assorted security services—roving military police, treasury guard, national police, commandos and the like—brandishing automatic weapons. But this overkill appeared as normal background after a short time, as it does in some other Latin American countries. Despite the unrest that Guatemala has gone through in recent years, as visitors, we never felt unsafe.

DAY TWO

We headed for Antigua Guatemala, the capital of a then-greater Guatemala (covering all of Central America) during the colonial era. To reach it, we left Guatemala City on Calzada Roosevelt, an extension of Boulevard Liberación (Diagonal 12). Whenever we were uncertain of our route, we simply asked for the road to Antigua.

On our way out through Zone 4, we passed through the large bus terminal and market, and got a good feel for the frenetic pace of small commerce in fruits, vegetables, pots, pans, hammocks, and dozens of other local necessities. When I bought a soda at a small stand, I noted a vendor slicing his hot dogs in two to make them go twice as far. Later, along Calzada Roosevelt, we noted a Pizza Hut, McDonald's, and assorted other fast food emporia where, no doubt, the hot dogs and hamburgers were served whole. If we had been so inclined, that would have been our last chance to savor modern fast food. For we were to find that this and most other surface Americanization did not exist past the limits of the capital.

From the outskirts of Guatemala City, the road climbs steadily to a pass. Traffic can be quite heavy, but fortunately, not dangerous. The road is divided, and there is a lane for slow trucks, which is hardly used. The shoulder is also paved in parts, and can be cycled. Traffic is especially heavy until the suburb of Mixco, then lightens somewhat. Along the way are good views down to Guatemala City, spread out along an axis of commercial buildings in a long valley, with much room still for expansion. To the south, we could see the waters of butterfly-shaped Lake Amatitlán, and the fuming Pacaya volcano. A lookout point on the inbound side of the highway makes a good rest area.

From San Lucas Sacatepéquez, a good, divided highway runs south from the Pan American Highway toward Antigua. Traffic is sparse, so the enchanting views of forest, hillside farming plots, roadside villages, looming volcanoes, and the old colonial capital lying at end of the twisting valley, can be safely appreciated. The entire run is downhill, and easy.

It took two hours to climb to San Lucas Sacatepéquez, the junction for the road to Antigua, at kilometer 30. From the Hotel Plaza, it took us about four and a half hours to reach Antigua, a distance of about 50 kilometers.

Antigua Guatemala is a pleasant, quiet town, one of the nicest I have seen in Latin America. Destroyed in a series of earthquakes, the city was virtually abandoned for more than a century. Now, the ruins of many of the colonial churches, palaces and homes have been authentically restored, and the streets are paved with cobblestones—a genuine touch, but one that makes for bumpy cycling.

As it was still the holiday period, most hotels were full. Among the dozens of hotels in town are the Posada de Don Rodrigo in a restored colonial mansion, $30 double and a good value for near-luxury accommodations. We settled, however, for the Hotel Belén, located near the Church of San Francisco and operated by nuns of the Belén (Bethlehem) order. Here we paid less than $10 for a comfortable double room, and healthy meals were only $3—the best value of our entire trip. On the edge of town, the Belén is perfect for cyclists—convenient to the roads, and secure. From it, we could see the three volcanoes that loom over Antigua: Agua, Acatenango, and active, fuming Fuego, its sparks and flames orange against the night.

On the square of Antigua, we found a detailed map for sale at a shop called Un Poco de Todo. This was a real find, as we had arrived in Guatemala City on New Year's Day, and had left without waiting for the geographical institute to re-open.

DAY THREE

We spent another night in pleasant Antigua, and made it the base for day trips. It was on this day that we began to appreciate our mountain bikes, as we drove on roads in a variety of conditions. Most were paved, but maintenance was poor, and when we hit potholes obscured in the shade of the coffee plantations that surround Antigua, our mountain bikes remained stable and undamaged.

We went to San Antonio Aguas Calientes. The road is paved from Antigua toward Ciudad Vieja. Four kilometers out, following the signpost, we turned right onto an unpaved route covered in powdery, black volcanic sand. Travelling all the time through coffee plantings, the bean-bearing shrubs shaded by taller, leafy trees, we ascended gently for another four kilometers, then rolled down a steep hill onto the main square of San Antonio. The village is noted for its exquisite, colorful weaving in geometric patterns. At stalls all around the town center, we were able to watch Indian women at work on simple looms, secured at one end to a tree and at the other end to their backs. Surely, it is cheaper even for these poor people to buy machine-made cloth than to laboriously create these rich fabrics, and yet the craft obviously is flourishing. Blouses, tablecloths, and assorted items made both locally and in neighboring towns were on sale; in many cases, the unique design in the fabric identified where it was made.

There are numerous other little villages spread out in the pocket valleys near Antigua, reached by roads and trails. We chose to ascend the hill we had just rolled down, turn right, and take a different unpaved road three kilometers toward Ciudad Vieja.

Even older than Antigua, Ciudad Vieja was an earlier capital of colonial Guatemala, but was destroyed in a volcanic eruption. Hardly anything remains of the original town. From Ciudad Vieja, the road is paved back to Antigua.

The triangular trip from Antigua to San Antonio Aguas Calientes and Ciudad Vieja and back to Antigua took about three and a half hours—an easy afternoon outing.

DAY FOUR

We left Antigua Guatemala at about 8:30 a.m., following the road toward Chimaltenango, a trip of about two-and-a-half hours. The way is a gentle upward slope as far as Parramos, passing through several huddled villages, such as Pastores, each dominated by an old church. There were also several large old beneficios, or processing centers, each a rambling collection of open, thick-walled structures with red tiled roofs, and concrete platforms for drying the coffee beans, as well as other areas for sorting, washing and husking. The road is narrow, but this is a quiet area and back route, with little traffic.

Near Pastores, we stopped to rest, and to chat with kids who, on their way to the Sunday market, were pausing to play at the local dump. The kids had plastic bags, just like bags you might carry from a store, but instead of buying things, they were filling them with garbage from the dump.

From Parramos, the road descends slightly to a small lake, then climbs back up toward the Pan American Highway at Chimaltenango.

Our next goal was the village of Panajachel, on Atitlán, a lake called by some the most beautiful in the world. Two routes were available. One, leaving the Pan American Highway at kilometer 69, is through the villages of Patzica and Patzún, a thin, paved road that drops into and climbs out of several narrow river valleys, before coming to Godínez, overlooking the lake from the east. We chose the high road, so to speak, the Pan American Highway, which climbs through the mountains north of the lake. Either route meant a journey of more than 100 kilometers from Antigua.

We could have stayed in a basic hotel in Chimaltenango and covered the stretch in two days. But Chimaltenango appeared to be of little interest for us. Considering the several mountain passes to be crossed, we decided that discretion was the better part of valor. We took a bus.

We waited about four minutes for a westbound bus to appear, and flagged it down. Considering some of the cargo that goes on top of these vehicles—bundles of piglets, hundred-pound sacks of corn, engines for small vehicles—it's no surprise that our bikes didn't cause the driver's helper to bat an eyelash.

In about an hour we reached the roadside hamlet of Zaculeu, near kilometer 115, at a frigid point on the highway nearly 3000 meters high. It looked to be a good point to hit the road again. A roadside mirador, or viewpoint, offered a stunning vista through a cleft in the mountains, down a wide valley to the surface of Lake Atitlán, glittering in the sun and stretching back between volcanoes in the distance. We simply indicated our desire to the driver, and he stopped to let us off. The fare was less than $3 for each person and bicycle.

Again on our bicycles, we followed the highway, winding gently down to Los Encuentros junction, turning off just beyond at kilometer 130 to a branch road to the south. We could feel the altitude in the cool, crisp air, invigorating, but short of oxygen. Eight twisting, mostly descending kilometers later, past corn fields withered in the dry season, and occasional terraced plots of onions and carrots irrigated by diverted mountain streams, and we were at the town of Sololá, on a cliff 600 meters directly above Lake Atitlán. We continued, gripping and releasing brake levers, passing successive waterfalls and admiring the variation on the lake view and volcanoes.

After another eight kilometers the road dropped us down into the lakeside garden town of Panajachel, with its villas with laboriously tended grounds, whitewashed Indian ranchos, and accommodations for visitors of all levels.

It took us about two hours to get to Panajachel from where the bus left us on the Pan American Highway, all on paved roads in good condition. There was little traffic on the branch road to the lake, but we had to take care, especially on curves, as there was not always room for two vehicles to meet and pass, and we could easily have been squashed in the middle of such an encounter. Even the Pan American Highway in this region sees few vehicles other than buses and a few trucks, making it pleasant for biking. I estimate that a continuous trip from Antigua would have taken more than fourteen hours—certainly a difficult day's journey, considering the several climbs and descents of over a thousand meters, but also quite impractical during the dry season, with fewer hours of daylight.

Panajachel offers a variety of accommodations, and for as little as four dollars the visitor can find a clean bed in a pension frequented by budget travellers. We saw no point in not staying along the shore of the most beautiful lake in the world, however, and checked in at the older and distinguished Hotel Tzanjuyú. For $20 we had a room with an unsurpassable view of the misty and mysterious lake. Another good value that we found was the Rancho Grande, $12 for a comfortable double room, though the location is a couple of hundred meters from the lake. The Hotel Monterrey charges only $8 in its substantial but neglected lakeside building, while the Hotel del Lago, newest and largest on the lake, charges less than $25. And there are many more bargains than these. We had good meals at the Fonda del Sol, on the main street; La Laguna, with its fireplace, a welcome feature on cool evenings; and the dining room of the Hotel Galindo.

Panajachel has a bank, but curiously, the tellers preferred travellers checks and refused to exchange our American cash. We were not inconvenienced, however. The soldier on duty at the door saw our problem, slung his submachine gun onto his shoulder, pulled out a roll of bills, and gave us a good rate—exactly what the bank was paying on travellers checks.

DAY FIVE

We met a curious assortment of people in and around Panajachel, some of them foreigners who were making a life and living in the village. One American sold plants and herbs out of a shop—mostly to other long-term visitors, I am sure—along with large, colorful birds fashioned from fabric. Others did I don't know what, but they seemed comfortable in their surroundings.

We spent the day out of the saddle, taking a boat trip across the lake to the village of Santiago Atitlán. The fare was about $4 for those who boarded at the Hotel Tzanjuyú, less for those who boarded at the public beach.

Santiago Atitlán is a more remote village than Panajachel, reached on a 15-kilometer crossing that brought us into the shadow of the three lake volcanoes—Atitlán, Toliman and San Pedro—and also, it seemed, a thousand years into the past. On the boat, we chatted with a former Peace Corps nurse who had worked in villages around the lake, tourists from Spain, and a bearded, aging, unkempt American who claimed to be an anthropologist.

The first inhabitants we saw were villagers fishing in the bay from a kind of boat built up from rough planks. These craft were small, with room for one person only, and reminded me of the kayaks I have seen used by the Inuit in northern Quebec. Curiously, the name of these boats, cayuco, is similar, and perhaps linguistically related. Near the wharf, women were scrubbing clothes in the shallows, and bathing themselves while keeping modestly covered.

The village has its own peculiar and strikingly beautiful outfits—the women's blouses and mens trousers, both striped in purple and white, are covered with intricately embroidered animals, especially birds. Many houses are of stone, and most are in compounds marked by walls of stone. Stone, in fact, is everywhere in the fields around town, and not surprisingly, given the towering volcanoes that have supplied it. The town is poor, but not in a grinding, depressing way. There is the social cohesion of an intact, traditional way of life.

From the south shore, the view to the north was totally different from what we had seen from Panajachel: a massive ridge, broken by river valleys, the broad delta of each the site of a separate village, with its own dialect and style of dress.

Travellers with mountain bikes can make a more extensive and interesting excursion than the one we took on this day. After crossing the lake on boat, the cyclist can continue from Santiago Atitlán on a dusty, bumpy road that parallels the south shore of the lake, under the twin volcanoes Atitlán and Toliman, to the village of San Lucas Toliman. From San Lucas, an excellent but little-trafficked highway from the coast climbs to Godínez, high above the northeast corner of the lake, and the old main highway leads back down to San Andres Semetabaj and Panajachel. This would be a leisurely full-day trip. One can also circumnavigate the lake in the opposite direction by a combination of dirt roads—one of which climbs high onto the slopes of the volcano San Pedro—and boats.

DAY SIX

Still using Panajachel as our base, we took a day trip on bicycle along the north shore of the lake to the villages of Santa Catarina Palopó and San Antonio Palopó. The dirt road was in quite poor condition, even though it was the dry season, but the views of volcanoes, as the road wound up and down from lake level and around mountains thrusting down into the water, were worth the effort of pedalling. The distances were not too long, and there were ascents of only two steep hills. The dusty surface—two inches deep in parts—caused numerous skids. Be careful! The only way to negotiate these roads is with a mountain bike, or with the heavy, thick-tired, one-speed bicycles used by a few natives.

In Santa Catarina, thirsty, we gave some business to a mother and daughter who operated an orange stand. Selling oranges would seem to be a rather straightforward business, but here it was an operation of some finesse. The orange was placed on a machine that subjected it with a prong at each pole, then a handle was turned, and the globe was skinned ever so continuously, artistically, by a whirling blade, leaving one long ribbon of skin snaking to the ground. The daughter was being trained in the business. We usually found vendors of peeled oranges at highway junctions, in markets, wherever people congregated and passed through in numbers. But in dusty Santa Catarina, we must have been the only customers all day.

Our round-trip distance for the day was 24 kilometers. Travelling slowly and cautiously, we left at 11 a.m. and were back in Panajachel at 4 p.m., with time spent looking around the two villages. Each is in its own lakeside canyon, the upper slopes used for corn plots, and the lower, terraced slopes given over to vegetables irrigated by splashing water directly from the lake, or from diverted mountain streams. At the very bottom of these natural amphitheaters were clusters of adobe houses.

DAY SEVEN

We traveled to Chichicastenango. Since we had cycled part of the route already, we took a bus uphill to Los Encuentros junction on the Pan American Highway. It took us 45 minutes to ascend, a distance of sixteen kilometers, starting from the Texaco station on the way out of Panajachel, where all buses stop. Fare was less than $1 per person with bicycle. I think it would take about three and a half hours to bicycle this distance, all of it uphill, and much of it quite steep.

Los Encuentros was a beehive of activity. Buses travelling the Pan American Highway stopped to discharge and pick up passengers, and allow those staying aboard to snack at roadside huts and relieve themselves in the bushes. There is no town, just a gasoline station and a post office. The small-time commerce was watched over by members of the civil defense patrols—Indian men wielding machetes and old rifles, in everyday work clothes, looking uncomfortable and not very competent. Some priests, walking along the road, assured us, in response to our inquiries, that the area was not dangerous, despite the armed presence.

From Los Encuentros, we covered the 17 kilometers to Chichicastenango on our bikes. We had been warned about a deep canyon on the way, but it was not as challenging as we had been led to believe. We had no trouble getting back up from the bottom—there are numerous switchbacks that make the climb more gentle than it appears from the top. Along the first five kilometers of the road, which were straight, we saw a lot of soldiers and civil guards. The temperature was quite cool. At kilometer 135, we stopped for an extraordinary view of Chichicastenango, and in the far distance, Santa Cruz del Quiché, each town perched on a hilltop and surrounded by canyons.

We had expected to be bothered by hustlers of various sorts in Chichicastenango, which has a reputation as a place that all the tourists visit. But on our arrival, the day before one of the twice-weekly markets, we found the town subdued. It is cooler than Panajachel, though about 300 meters below the level of frosty Los Encuentros.

The Mayan Inn, with well-appointed rooms off courtyards in a series of converted old homes, charged less than $30 for a double room. It was highly recommended, and we stayed there and found it charming. But we should have asked for more wood for our fireplace. Our room was damp and quite cold. Rates were similar at the new but nevertheless atmospheric Hotel Santo Tomás. Cheaper was the Pension Chugnilá, $10 double, with fireplaces in some rooms. All are near the main square where the market is held. There are several cheaper lodging places as well, none especially recommendable.

After checking in at our hotel in the afternoon, we had time to walk to the Pascual Abaj, a stone idol on a ridge above town. On the way, passing through a house where fiesta costumes are warehoused, some children beckoned to us, then disappeared into dressing rooms, and reappeared in ceremonial costumes as grotesque Spanish conquistadores and proud native chieftains. They danced for us as well, a playful performance for the visitor that contained a full measure of pride in their traditions.

DAY EIGHT

We spent the morning, a Thursday, at the market in "Chichi." It is essential to arrive in time to see the Thursday or Sunday markets, which are the fame of this town, when inhabitants of the surrounding countryside come in to transact business with itinerant merchants from all over. Much of the merchandise is utilitarian, crude furniture and the like, but the textiles are extraordinary, as they are everywhere in Guatemala.

After lunch we left for Santa Cruz del Quiché, one canyon removed. This was a troubled area in recent years—guerrilla raids and sweeps by the army took place—but we saw nothing to indicate that problems continue. The road is paved, scenic, and not difficult to cover on bicycle, though we had to watch out for potholes. Our time to Santa Cruz del Quiché was two and a half hours.

Among hotels in Santa Cruz del Quiché, which sees few tourists from outside, is the San Pascual, which is clean and basic, $4 double with a cold shower in the room. We stayed there, and had no complaints. Even without a fireplace, our room was warmer than the one at the Mayan Inn, perhaps due to a combination of lower altitude, and concrete-block walls that held the heat of the day. The Posada de la Calle Real charged $9 for small, clean double rooms, with hot water in a shared bath. Despite its pretentious name ("Inn of the Royal Street"), it did not seem as good as the San Pascual.

There are some small eating-places in Santa Cruz del Quiché—one can't really call them restaurants—but this was one of the few places in Guatemala where our stomachs judged that we should cook for ourselves. We broke out the alcohol stove and the freeze-dried food, and lightened our supplies.

After checking in at our hotel, we made a side trip to Gumarcaj, the site of the capital of one of the pre-Conquest Indian nations of Guatemala. The road is gravel and dirt, but was not difficult, especially without our luggage, though we had our usual caution for potholes. The entrance to the ruins is about four kilometers from town on the right side. There's no sign, but a street light marks the spot. If you reach a descent into a canyon, you know you've gone too far. (Guess how I know.) Ask people if you are not sure. There's always someone around in rural Guatemala, so it's easy to check if you're going the right way. The archaeological site appears at first to be not too impressive, but a model of the original city helps to identify features of the site. Local kids will open the little building where the model is located. They deserve a small tip.

One unpleasant little surprise in our hotel was the 220-volt electrical service. As the outlets were of the kind used in Canada and the U.S., I nearly burned out my electric razor. It would be a good idea to check the voltage before you plug anything in.

DAY NINE

We left Santa Cruz del Quiché very early in the morning on the direct road to Totonicapán. As we were to find out, this road is unpaved, in poor condition, and hardly trafficked at all. Buses going between the two towns return to the Pan American Highway, travelling twice the distance of the direct route, but probably in a much shorter time, and with less wear and tear. There are no accommodations of any kind along the way. If you take this road—and do it only in the dry season—do not under any circumstances leave later than 6:15 a.m., or you will run the risk of spending the night in the cold away from any lodging place. Do not count on finding a lift at nightfall. Bring food and beverages for the day—about one and a half liters of liquid per person. We spotted only two places selling soft drinks.

The first six kilometers out of Quiché were gravel in moderately good condition. At six kilometers, the road plunged into a canyon, and we reached some hot springs, which are common in this part of Guatemala. The road follows the canyon for about seven kilometers, all of it gradual ascent. Along the way are numerous little pools of hot water seeping from the earth, and it was fascinating to see people washing their clothes and themselves as naturally as we would use our tubs and washing machines. Fish inhabited some of the pools, no doubt a quite specialized ecosystem.

Toward the end of the canyon is the intersection for a road to the village of San Antonio Ilotenango, after which the road rises quite steeply, to a high plateau that appears to be populated mostly by Indians living traditionally. Surrounding us on all sides were fields of corn stalks withered in the dry season—corn is the major crop, no doubt with a serious ecological impact from its monoculture. There are several side roads—inquire to make sure that you are following the road to Totonicapán. Posts along the way indicate the distance in kilometers to the summit of a pass four kilometers outside of Totonicapán.

In Guatemala, you are never really alone in the countryside. If there is a road, people are using it, often on foot. And we kept encountering them, in a way that repeatedly made me feel like a Martian. It was hot, I was without a tee-shirt, cycling along ahead of my partner. A child, a woman, a man would be ahead, and, on seeing me, would take off into the nearest corn field. At first, I, too, was terrified. Were they running from terrorists? From soldiers? Should I hide or turn back? No, it happened again, and again. They were running from me, the white man on bicycle. Never in Latin America had I scared the inhabitants. Had there been an incident involving armed men on bicycles or motorcycles? How different had it been when the conquistador appeared on horseback?

From kilometer 17, after crossing the plateau, to kilometer 9, the road ascended again, gradually, and was in increasingly bad shape. From kilometer 9 to kilometer 0, we had to walk from three to four kilometers, because of the grade and the ruts and rocks of the road. Views to valleys on both sides are impressive. Nearing the summit, we had another close encounter, with a mother and her children. There was no place for these poor people to flee—the verges of the road were cliffs. They dropped their huge sacks of grain from their backs and stared at us in terror. We accelerated over the rocks.

From kilometer 0, we descended to Totonicapán. But the road was still poor. Take care!

Totonicapán is a center for weaving, pottery making, and assorted other crafts, the products of which can be seen in the market and at several shops. There are several small hotels, but we chose to continue downhill, on a good paved road with little traffic, to Cuatro Caminos junction on the Pan American Highway. From there, it's a ten-kilometer ride to Quezaltenango, the second-largest city of Guatemala. As it was getting late, we boarded a bus, but even in daytime I would recommend against bicycling the route. Traffic is quite heavy between Quezaltenango and the several small towns nearby on the main road. Bus fare into town was less than a dollar, waiting time less than two minutes.

Total distance from Quiché to Totonicapán is 45 kilometers. It took us eight and a half hours. The twelve kilometers to the Pan American Highway took another hour. On this last stretch we noted some warm springs swimming pools off to the right, but we didn't have time to stop.

In Quezaltenango, the best hotel is the Bonifaz, just off the main square, where service and accommodations are impeccable, and the rate is just $20 double. The restaurant is recommended.

DAY TEN

We stayed in Quezaltenango, seeing a number of sites in this rather staid and dignified highland city. Easily visited is a park high on a hill overlooking the town center. There are several natural hot springs above the city as well, from which you can step out into air that is often brisk and invigorating. Quezaltenango's market is large and fascinating. The city is dominated by the volcano Santa María, which erupts periodically.

If you have the time, it would be worthwhile to stay a few days in Quezaltenango in order to visit the nearby villages, which specialize in various handicrafts, such as furniture-making and weaving. The tourist office on the main square is quite helpful in orienting visitors.

DAY ELEVEN

We went from Quezaltenango to the Fuentes Georginas hot springs spa, a most pleasant ride up a scenic road through highland tropical forest. Two routes are available out of Quezaltenango; I recommend the one via the town of Cantel, through which we passed on Sunday, the very active market day. An unpaved road leads up from the highway to Cantel from a point two kilometers to the north; a second, shorter road—a foot trail, really, made of steps cut into the hillside—leads back down, giving you the choice of not retracing your path. I went up to the market in Cantel; my companion ran into the director of a hospital in Guatemala City, and the two chatted about medical matters for an hour. The hospital director gave us a load of oranges for the road.

We reached Cantel in 45 minutes from Quezaltenango, and Zunil, a village noted for its weaving, in another 25 minutes. The highway was mostly flat. The unpaved road to the Fuentes Georginas runs for eight and a half kilometers from the main highway, from a point across the highway from Zunil. The road is in good condition, and we reached the springs in an hour and a half.

The hotel at the Fuentes Georginas has seen better days, and can now only be described as basic. Rates are only $6 double, and you should tip the personnel to bring you wood for your fireplace—you'll need it to keep warm! The altitude is about 3000 meters. And bring your own food—the restaurant is quite bad. Once again, we broke out our stove and food supplies. Though things could have been more tidy, we enjoyed staying at a place that once was quite elegant, soaking in the hot-springs pools, watched over by a Roman-style statue missing an arm, gazing down at the expanses of rich and intensely farmed valleys below. It felt like a Roman resort, but for the indigenous people of the vicinity, whose presence reminded us that this was all uniquely Guatemalan.

DAY TWELVE

From the Fuentes Georginas, we rolled back down to Zunil and the paved highway, which continues to the coastal lowlands. We passed a toll booth, but nobody came out to request payment, and continued down, down, down, from slopes planted with corn, past areas of vegetable gardens, through coffee country. We had to brake intermittently, and watch out for potholes in an otherwise easy road. Along the way are several fuming hot springs, in the vicinity of Santa María de Jesús and the Santa María volcano. Traffic in the morning was light to moderate.

Eight kilometers past Santa María is a paved branch road to the right, to El Palmar, another five kilometers distant, and already in the hot country. Views of the Santiaguito volcano, which erupted onto the slopes of Santa María in 1902 and has been active ever since, are good. El Palmar was partially destroyed by volcanic activity about five years ago, but the village is still inhabited. Better views are to be had by securing your bicycle and walking for about ten minutes to a broad river, which is crossed by a 300-meter suspension bridge for foot traffic only. Return to the main highway on the same road on which you came—your map may show another road, which is in very bad condition.

We continued down a more gentle grade, until we reached the Pacific Highway. Turning right, we followed the main road west for three kilometers. A fork offered us the choice of going around San Felipe, or the shorter route through the town. We chose the latter, of course, negotiated the narrow streets lined with houses of rough planks, turned left at the church, and continued back toward the main road, descending all the way.

We stopped for the night at the excellent Hotel La Colonia, outside of Retalhuleu, paying about $14 for a double room.

We enjoyed the swimming pool, and our first contact with the hot tropical lowlands of Guatemala.

DAY THIRTEEN

We realized immediately that the Pacific Highway was not at all, but not at all, suitable for long-distance bicycle touring. The heavy traffic of all sorts of trucks as well as buses on the flat, two-lane road makes it impossible to ride safely. I recommend that you stay away from the Pacific Highway except for short stretches. We decided to end the cycling part of our trip, and rode on into Retalhuleu for a look around a bustling, hot city.

From Retalhuleu we took a bus back to Guatemala City. Fare: $3 per person, less than $2 per bike.

We spent more time touring Guatemala City, but the most interesting part of our trip was behind us.

By the time I took my Guatemala trip, I had worked out most of the bugs in planning and executing my Latin American bicycle tours. My big regret is that I did not have more time. I would have liked to take more day trips from Quezaltenango, to San Marcos and other highland towns; to see more of the villages around Lake Atitlán; to have made a few more excursions off the paved highways.

Perhaps on another visit I'll ride north of Santa Cruz del Quiché, on the main gravel "highway" to Sacapulas, and the great mountain ridge along the Chixoy River. I'll take camping equipment, and circle back to Guatemala City by way of Huehuetenango or Cobán. But these are not routes for the casual cyclist.

Even in a short time, one learns a lot about Guatemala, about the ways of its Indian peoples, and even about volcanoes. Guatemala gets a top rating as a bicycling destination.

11
YUCATAN AND BELIZE

Here's a trip that is almost totally flat, until you get to western Belize. If you've never gone bicycle touring before, this would be a good first outing. There are no great physical challenges, there are acceptable lodging places within an easy day's ride of each other, and buses ply the roads fairly frequently, so you can get a ride if you overdo it or have a mechanical problem.

You're probably thinking that you could find such an unchallenging excursion without travelling thousands of miles from home. Fair enough. But there are other attractive aspects to a Yucatan-Belize trip.

If you're interested in swimming and/or diving, you'll find some of the best beaches and coral reefs in the world.

Archeological sites abound in both Yucatan and Belize. If you're interested enough, you can do nothing but cycle from Mayan ruin to Mayan ruin.

Or, the living cultures of today could be the high point of this trip. You will encounter the Mestizo and Maya in the Yucatan. You will find them in Belize as well, along with Mennonites, Creoles, Caribs, Chinese, and stray members of assorted other tribes.

YUCATAN & BELIZE CYCLING ROUTE

100   200 KILOMETERS

LATIN AMERICA ON BICYCLE ©2003

MEXICO

YUCATAN PENINSULA

Cancun

Puerto Morelos
Playa del Carmen
Akumal
Tulum

Cozumel

Felipe Carrillo Puerto

Bacalar
Chetumal

Corozal

CARIBBEAN SEA

Orange Walk

'Cay Caulker

San Ignacio
Benque Viejo

Belize City
BELMOPAN

BELIZE

GUATEMALA

HONDURAS

And, for someone who lives in the cold north, there is a lot of sun, and a predictable dry season. Well, nearly dry.

This can also be an inexpensive trip, if you arrive at and leave from Cancun. A high percentage of charter flights to Mexico head for that resort city. You can get a reasonably priced fare from almost any major city in the United States or Canada, without a change of planes for you and your bicycle (perhaps the latter is more important). And as Cancun is one of the destinations in Latin America closest to the United States, travel time is short.

You can get reasonable fares to Belize, as well—it's not all that far from the United States. But the round-trip deals to Cancun are so much better, that we started and ended our trip there. An open-jaw ticket, with a return from Belize City, would have cost twice our $300 Montreal-Cancun charter.

Though Belize and the Caribbean coast of Mexico are not densely populated, settlements or resorts are usually not more than fifty miles apart. So you don't have to overstretch your energies to get to your next stopping point. You have a choice of accommodations, from luxurious down to less than basic. Even camping is easily accomplished. In short, you can stay however you like almost wherever you like. There is no shortage of eating places, either.

Even the heavy touristic development in and near Cancun can be an advantage. If your Spanish is inadequate, you can use English almost everywhere along the Caribbean coast of Mexico. In Belize, which used to be called British Honduras, English is the official language. Of course, the downside is that you don't really feel that you're in Latin America, at least, not when you're close to Cancun. But the culture shock at the beginning of your trip is lessened.

As you go south, you get into places that are more genuinely Mexican, and different from home. And Belize, with its crazy-quilt combination of cultures, is different from anywhere you've been.

You're most definitely in the tropics on this route, but even at sea level, you won't see much dense jungle. Much of Yucatan is naturally scrub vegetation. The parts that were once forest were logged out long ago. In Belize, the roadside views are more varied and interesting. The seaside and seascape, however, are something else. The water is warm, the beaches are perfect, and the fish and coral, in their multiplicity of color and form, are stupendous.

My companion and I spent six days in Quintana Roo, the Mexican state that encompasses the eastern coast of the Yucatan. From Chetumal, we entered Belize, where we spent another seven days, before re-tracing our route by bus. This was my companion's first Latin American bicycle trip, and this route made for an easy entry.

You have to choose your month of travel with some care. In general, there's more rain the farther south you go. Belize City and the area to the north have a definite dry season, from November or December to May. If you go from February to April, you're practically assured of good weather, though April is the hottest month. In May and June, and from August to October, you can have bad weather, but it's not too trying compared to the extremes of Europe or North America. From mid-November to the end of January, there are occasional storms. We went in January, which is considered a dry month, if not the height of the dry season. We were not too lucky. It was the worst January in many a year. Still, it wasn't terrible. We got wet.

In Yucatan, for the first time in Latin America, I met other visitors on bicycle. They, in turn, had met many others. So there are a number of votes for bicycle travel in this area. In Belize, though we didn't meet other cyclists, many hotel proprietors told us that we were not the first touring cyclists they had seen.

Though we went only to the eastern coast of the Yucatan, there are many other places of interest in the peninsula—the city of Merida, and the archeological sites of Chichen Itzá and Cobá, for example. The roads are flat and good, and it wouldn't be hard to make a circle trip from Cancun, or from Merida, for that matter.

In Belize, it's impossible to make a loop by bicycle. The only good road runs from the Mexican border to Belize City, then west to Guatemala. There are poor roads to the south. Unless you're continuing to Guatemala on a dirt road, you'll have to re-trace your route, by bicycle or bus. Because the country is so small, this won't take long. You can go from the western end of Belize all the way back to Cancun in a day, with lucky bus connections. And you'll get a new perspective on where you've been as you do so.

As for guidebooks, I recommend the South American Handbook and Chicki Mallan's *Yucatan Handbook* (Moon Publications)—not one or the other, but both—neither is complete. For Belize, Paul Glassman's *Belize Guide*, recently updated and expanded, is your most useful source for pre-trip and on-the-road information. Use the genuine Passport Press edition. (An edition by another publisher contains numerous errors.) A map of the state of Quintana Roo is available at no charge from the airport tourist office in Cancún. It is detailed and useful, with locations of all towns clearly marked, along with symbols to indicate available facilities. And it's free.

For Belize, you can use the map in Glassman's guide, though the official Tourist Facilities Map is quite detailed and useful. We bought a copy in Corozal, in northern Belize, for about $3. It can also be ordered from the Belize Tourist Board, Box 325, Belize City. The ITMB map, published in Vancouver, Canada, is also good.

DAY ONE

Our charter flight left at 6 a.m., which meant we had to be at the airport two hours before. It was a short night. Preparation of our baggage was simplified: unlike scheduled flights, charters don't carry any cargo. Nobody will charge you to bring your bicycle, or worry about an extra item of baggage. I didn't have to tape my bicycle bags together to make them into one piece of luggage.

The on-board service was good, but it was also the kind of flight where they offer you a beer at 7 a.m. We preferred sleep.

When we arrived, I looked around, there were more than ten other flights arriving at the same time, with hordes of tourists. I was expecting hours and hours of waiting, with legendary Mexican inefficiency. But it didn't work out that way. The airport is built quite simply, all on one level, and we could look out and see the baggage handlers open the belly compartments and take out the luggage and send the carts right into the terminal, where we picked up our bags and bikes. In less than half an hour, we had cleared all formalities, exchanged some money, and were on our way out of the airport. It was January 2.

The only thing I know about the meaning of Cancun is that "can" means "four" in Maya. It says so in Mallan's guide. I wondered my whole trip as to the significance of "cun," but that was the extent of my curiosity about the place. We later cycled the whole peninsula and Cancun Island, which is securely tied to the mainland by bridges.

Cancun, for the cyclist, is merely a point of arrival and departure. If your plane arrives late, you can find a hotel, if you don't want to cycle on to Puerto Morelos, 20 kilometers to the south, which is as far from the airport as is the center of Cancun. There's a nice beach, and there are five hotels, with more under construction. An alternative strategy is to go north through Cancun to Puerto Juarez, and by ferry to Isla Mujeres.

If you are returning from Cancun, you can leave Isla Mujeres for the end. It's a nice, small island, with one road, which you can explore in a leisurely fashion.

Another excursion that I would recommend, without your bike, is to Isla Contoy, a bird sanctuary.

There are lots of accommodations in Cancun, and the hotels downtown are cheaper than those on the beach strip. But everything is getting more and more expensive, despite what is said about the continuing Mexican economic crisis. Cancun and vicinity, for all purposes, are part of the American economy. There's even a customs checkpoint between the rest of Mexico and the resort area.

If it's really late, and you don't mind spending some money, you can go to the Club Mediterranee, which is near the south end of the Cancun peninsula. The charge is about

$100 per person per day, the beach is nice, meals and wine and sports are included, and you're away from the noise and high pressure of the main strip.

If you arrive late and go into Cancun for the night, I would suggest that you not bother to assemble your bicycle. Put it, still dismantled, into a taxi. With tie straps, two can go into the trunk even of a little Datsun. It's not safe to face the heavy traffic between the airport and town, not just because it's night, but also because you've just come off some stressful airline travel. With no shoulder on the highway, you're better off waiting until daylight. The fare should be less than $10 to any hotel—make sure it's set before you go anywhere. Most drivers will try to get as much as they can. Around Cancun, people see you not as a tourist, or a human being, but as a bag of green stuff. I'm sure that many of those taxi drivers make a very good living, not only for Mexico, but by North American standards as well.

We arrived about 10:30 a.m. local time, which is an hour earlier than Montreal time. Just when you leave the airport, there is a little restaurant, where you can have a drink or a snack, and get accustomed to the temperature, which is quite warm. There's a nice terrace, and even with the noise of taxis and buses, it's a nice place to stop. You can even finish assembling your bike, and dismantle it here on your way home. You're at sea level in Cancun, not in the cool highland tropics of Guatemala City or San José. It's a shock, especially when you're coming from a huge snowstorm and temperatures of minus 15 Centigrade (5 Fahrenheit). We didn't crack from the temperature change, anyway.

We headed south, toward Puerto Morelos. We had already been as far as Cozumel by other means of transportation, but it was different on bicycle. The airport is about 2.5 kilometers from Highway 307, the main and only north-south road along the coast. Once you get to the highway and turn off the showcase airport access road, the shoulder disappears.

We applied sunscreen cream, but soon the clouds rolled in, and we didn't see any sun at all. I must tell you that for the whole trip, we did not get what they call normal weather for this time of year. January is generally a dry month, but we had some showers. In fact, by the middle of that day, we had some heavy ones. It was like taking a hot shower at home. I had nearly left my raincoat at home, but I finally gave in to my own advice, and packed it.

Traffic southward was light to medium—not so heavy that we had to concentrate totally on the road, rather than what was around us. The pavement is in excellent condition. The road is exactly two lanes wide, with uncut brush growing right to the pavement. Your reflective safety vest is a must. The most interesting moments come when two buses travelling in opposite directions meet and pass, just at the point where you happen to be. Whoosh. Don't ride too close to the bushes, or try to see the snakes sunning themselves along the roadside.

About 10 kilometers south of the airport, on the east side of the road, is a place called Crocodile Park. It's a good place to stop and see hundreds of crocodiles. I can predict what your dreams will be on the night that you visit. It costs about $5 to get in.

At the intersection for Puerto Morelos is the first gas station that you will encounter. You can inflate your tires, if your pump did not do an adequate job.

Puerto Morelos is a nice place. Several persons had recommended the Posada Amor to us, and with a suggestive name like that—Love Inn—we checked it out. By the time you read this, there will be many more hotels open. There is a boat from Puerto Morelos to Cozumel, we were told at the airport that departure time is 10 a.m. It's worth verifying the current schedule as soon as you arrive. But as we had a good amount of daylight ahead of us, we decided, after a look around, to continue to Playa del Carmen, which is about 45 kilometers from the airport.

Playa del Carmen is much more of a resort than Puerto Morelos. In fact, the beach is quite, quite nice, with crystalline blue waters stretching away toward Cozumel Island, shaded by palms. When I was last there, three years before, there was nothing special about the place, but Playa del Carmen has been cleaned up, there are some attractive restaurants and hotels, and you could pass a few pleasant days there.

We had dinner, then took the passenger ferry from Playa del Carmen to Cozumel island. They used to have just one big, slow vessel on this run, crossing four or five times a day, but now there are large, medium and small vessels, providing fast, medium and slow service to the island. We took the jet boat for just over a dollar. There was no charge for our bicycles, we were told at the ticket office, though the guy who took our bicycles aboard did try to get some money from us.

If you go on this boat, try not to be seen by a policeman. Technically, it's for passengers only. The jet boat is making so much competition that the other operators keep an eye on it. The slow boats charge just as much. We left Playa del Carmen at 8 p.m. The boat goes very fast—it's built in Norway—and we reached Cozumel in just 25 minutes, compared to two hours on the old boats. Everybody rides inside and they close the door. You feel that you're in a plane. There's a big video screen inside, and they show clips of musical hits.

The landscape of Cozumel is not at all interesting—just scrub vegetation—and the town of San Miguel has nothing special to offer. If you go there, it is to bicycle along the sea. You can make a circle tour of the island, taking in a variety of sea views and shoreline features. The western side of the island is protected from the full force of the sea. There are no waves, and the sea is calm. On the other side, the waves are big and the sea can be tricky, so be careful if you swim there.

You have a large choice of hotels in Cozumel. You can pay a lot. If you want to pay $55 a night, you can go north or south of town—I think the Presidente and Sol Caribe, to the south, are the best. All hotels outside of the town face the beach. There are also some good ones downtown. We chose a budget hotel—about $25 double—called the Paraíso Caribe. It's a plain, adequate place., It was obvious that once it was built, it was decided to spend the minimum on maintenance. Too bad. With a little upkeep it could have been nice. It was near the airport, about seven minutes from the dock on bicycle. The location, away from town and the beach, might have been a disadvantage for others, but with a bicycle, no such problems existed. And it is quiet. We spent three nights there.

DAY TWO

We were quite tired from our first day, so we were not on our bicycles until 11 a.m. First we had breakfast at Los Moros, on Benito Juárez and Avenida 10. It's a popular place, which means it is probably safe. There's enough turnover that food does not have time to spoil.

I have to confess that I don't like Mexican food, at least, not in Mexico. I love it in Mexican restaurants at home. But in Mexico, I am afraid of getting sick, more so than in other countries, so I am especially cautious. And you can get sick quite easily.

We went biking around the hotel zone to the north of town. There isn't much of interest there, except for the marina, where private boats from all over the world dock. It's in a natural lagoon.

An interesting point about the weather: In the United States, Canada is where the cold air always come from, in the weather reports. In Mexico, it comes from the United States, which, for me, was a relief of sorts. People said they had been having some bad weather because of the "norte," the wind that blows from the north. I didn't quite understand the significance of the "norte" until that night, when the wind was so strong that we couldn't walk on the street. In fact, it looked like people walking in a hurricane.

We went south along the coast, and in that direction, we found some interesting beaches. I want to tell you that there is a place called La Caleta, near the Hotel Presidente, which is where most of the diving boats are based. Cozumel is rated as one of the best diving places in the world. If you're interested in diving, go to one of the diving shops in town. We went to the American-owned Dive Paradise, but there are others.

I would suggest for the first day that you go to Laguna Chankanab, which is what we did. This is a park that has been established by the Mexican government. It's sort of a state park, and one of the cleanest I have seen. There are changing rooms, and a nice, clean beach—all man-made from trucked-in sand. You can rent snorkeling equipment, and the landscaping is fantastic. They have built a botanical garden, with all sorts of flowers and plants, including bamboo. When you're in a bamboo thicket, it looks like big blades of grass, and you feel like an ant.

The water off Chankanab is crystal clear, warm, with no waves, and you can snorkel safely. It's full of fish of all colors. Just put on a mask and fins, and you will discover this world. It's about 12 kilometers from San Miguel. You can also rent equipment and go to the small Yokab reef offshore of Chankanab, or to another reef about a kilometer to the south. Snorkeling equipment costs $5 to rent, Scuba equipment about $20. You must have your diving certificate.

We took a 45-minute dive at Yukab reef, about 50 meters from the shore. It's a good place to go if you haven't been diving in some time. The water is very clear, quiet, and there are a lot of fish, and a reef to be seen.

Back in San Miguel, we had a fish plate for about $5 at Pato's Tacos, near the corner of 10 Avenida and Dr. Rosario Salas. There is decent wine in Mexico from Baja California, for a few dollars per bottle.

DAY THREE

This was the day of our island tour. It's 40 kilometers for the whole circle route, a good day's run without too much strain, and you can visit a lot of things.

A good strategy is to start across the island from San Miguel, then spend the rest of the day going around along the shore, taking breaks to swim every now and then. You go east for about six kilometers to a sign that points the way to the San Gervasio ruins, which are another eight kilometers down a side road. The road is flat, and paved all the way. Along the secondary road, you will see pipes, and pumping stations, and wells. This is where the water problem of San Miguel was solved.

People at the entrance to the ruins will guard your bicycle. You can give them a small tip. There are a certain number of structures, and you can walk around in the bush. Thirty minutes is sufficient time to see the ruins.

Continuing around the island, you will pass a series of beaches. You can stop and have a swim, but I will tell you that the beaches on the other side are more quiet, and there is no current. If you like to swim in the waves, the Chen Rio beach is very good.

Continuing on the paved road, you will pass the access road to the El Cedral ruins, three kilometers off the main route. Then you turn north, and come to another series of beaches on the western side of the island.

Playa San Francisco (San Francisco Beach) is a good place to stop and eat. There is one big restaurant. The beach is very nice, but a little bit crowded. You can continue a couple of kilometers to Playa Maya, which is like Playa San Francisco, but less frequented. You can dive here, though there is no coral reef. Between the two beaches, a road provides access to where organized diving tours take off. The best place to swim is Chankanab, near the end of the island loop. I always feel secure when there are a lot of fish that look at me as I swim.

This tour of the island seems to be very easy, but if you run into wind, it can take all day. So start early in the morning, before it gets too warm. You will see a lot of birds, crystal-clear water, and have an overall view of the island, and visit some ruins.

We had dinner at Pizza Rolandi, $20 for two. All prices on the menu were in U.S. dollars. It was good and clean, Swiss-run and with Swiss cleanliness.

DAY FOUR

This was a special day. we wanted to go back to Playa del Carmen. But, in the morning, we took a day dive. I don't want to keep hammering a point, but Cozumel is one of the best places in the world for diving, though it's quite expensive. If you go snorkeling and find it rewarding, you'll find diving many more times rewarding. Just as a bird book is essential to the birder, a book about coral and fish is essential to the diver. Various of these are sold in Cozumel, including one in a waterproof edition that your kids can read in the bathtub after you're done with it. You can identify what you see, and also find out which fish are dangerous. I can say that with some observation, you can see most of the fish in one of these books, if you go snorkeling in four or five places, which is quite a lot better than you can do with a bird book.

We went diving with the Dive Paradise company. For two dives and lunch, we paid $36, plus another $10 for equipment. The first dive is at 80 feet for a maximum of 35 minutes. We went near the Palancar reef. We swam through caves with a lot of fish inside. Their colors, and those of the coral, were fantastic. You go in small groups, six or seven people with one guide. There are no words to describe what you see. After lunch, the second dive is at 45 feet, for nearly an hour. The reefs are all different. For Natalie, my companion, it was her first dive after certification.

After our dives, we rode our bicycles to the main dock, and took the water jet boat back. There was supposed to have been a service to Cancun, as well as to Playa del Carmen, but for some reason having to do with the dock at Cancun, it didn't operate. Keep this latter route in mind, however, it can be a good alternative.

We had some bad weather, and for a certain time I was afraid that the jet boat would turn over.

In Playa del Carmen, there are many hotels. If you want to sleep out, just walk along the beach with your bicycle. Ask, and people will tell you where you can hang up your hammock, and spend the night with the noise of the waves. Lock up your bicycle. There are many cheap hotels. We stayed in a very nice one, the Playacar. In the off season, you might be able to bargain, but we had to spend about $65 double. We had a nice, breezy room off the beach, with excellent service. The architecture and decor are interesting, with extensive use of tiles, and great doors on the sea side that almost bring the beach right into your room.

For a quiet place not on the beach, try the Cabinas Nuevo Amanecer. The town is booming, and you can check out any number of hotels with your bicycle. I don't think space will be a problem, except during Christmas week.

Also in town, if you have dirty clothes, there is a place that washes all the linen of the hotels, you can bring your stuff there, they will charge about 20 cents per item. They have old-fashioned washing machines, half motor-, half human-powered. This is just at the entrance to the village, near the main road. Ask for the lavandería.

We had a very, very good meal at Al Baco. I ate Venetian chicken. They had lasagna and all that, and the owner was a real Roman. Playa del Carmen is a good place to stop and relax, it is becoming more pleasant every year.

DAY FIVE

I suggest that you leave early in the morning, let's say 8 or 9 a.m., because just after, all the tourist buses from Cancun descend on Tulum, using the same highway you're trying to ride on. The only traffic seems to be buses full of tourists. If you leave by 9 a.m., you will get to your next stopping point early enough in the day. We had only light traffic. Be very careful for buses and trucks passing each other.

From Playa del Carmen, you have a choice of destinations for the day, as well as stopping places for swims along the way. We decided on Akumal, which is about 30 kilometers down the coast. It would be two hours non-stop.

On that road there are many small advertisements for Coca. These refer to simple homes where families sell soft drinks as a sideline. If you want to visit a Maya family, the best thing is to stop at one of these houses for a drink. Some of them even have cenotes, natural wells that occur where the upper layer of limestone has caved in, revealing the water table underneath. They will be happy to show them to you. There are also beehives all along the road. You will see them every five or six kilometers. The vegetation along the road is jungly, but not too thick or dense. It is not the tropical rain forest of your imagination. The road is mostly straight. I think the way to go is to ride a bit, take the air, look for birds, see the jungle, stop for a Coke, then go off to another fantastic place to swim, or sunbathe, or visit some ruins.

You will pass a place called X-Caret, which is not to be confused with another X-Caret to the south. At the first, there is a restaurant. The more interesting X-Caret is the second one, but it's not identified on the road, though it's on the map. At Paamul, there are beaches, camping, and assorted other facilities. Then you come to Akumal.

We stopped at Akumal for two nights. I'll tell you why. Akumal is a small paradise, with one of the nicer beaches you will see anywhere, fringed by a coconut plantation that

171

provides plenty of shade. The lower parts of the trees are painted white. It is very clean, swept every day, three kilometers long. About 100 meters from the beach is a coral reef. So you have crystal-clear waters without waves. The snorkeling and scuba diving are fantastic. In just three feet of water you will see a lot of fish.

It is also, up to a certain point, expensive. We stayed at the Hotel Akumal Caribe, for $69 double for a room with sea view. As at other hotels, it was no hassle to bring our bicycles into our rooms. I think they know that bicycles are a good candidate for theft, so they do what they can to accommodate you. If you leave your bike in your hotel room, lock it. Of course, lock up your bike outside, no matter what people tell you, to a water pipe or something like that.

There are also small cabins with kitchenettes that you can rent for about $65 a day, and cram in about as many people as you would like—up to eight. You can also rent small houses by the beach. A country store at the entrance to the resort is well stocked with food, by Mexican standards.

We spent our first day at the beach.

Above all, Akumal is a diving center. You have the Mexican diving institute, and everything seems to be American-run. There isn't much choice of restaurants. The same person owns all of them. You're not robbed, but there are no bargains.

If you don't want to spend the relatively high prices of Akumal, you can continue to Tulum, another 27 kilometers down the road, and near which there are cheap accommodations. Between Akumal and Tulum, there are a number of attractions, which I will mention in a minute.

DAY SIX

In the morning we took the opportunity to go diving in undersea canyon formations. Akumal is a perfect combination of places to rent equipment, snorkel, dive, swim, sunbathe, or just relax.

Akumal is also a good place for day excursions. In the afternoon, we headed toward the second X-Caret, about eight kilometers to the south. You have to ask for it, as a sign on the road only reads Aventuras. There you will find a nice and clear cenote which is supposed to have fresh water, though how this can be so close to the sea, I do not know. I would suppose that there is a certain percentage of salt water. The water is so clear that you don't see it, just the reflection of the rock face and the shade above it, it is a perfect optical illusion. There are also Mayan ruins very near, and a small beach, very good for swimming. You can also swim in the cenote. I won't say anything more except that there are very interesting things. I will let you discover the rest.

If you continue, about three kilometers to the south, you will come to a place called Xel-Ha. Personally, I like to swim in safe places, where there are a lot of people, so that if there is something dangerous like a big fish, I will not be the one to see it first. Xel-Ha lagoon is full of people and colorful fish. If you like more quiet, you can ask at Akumal for a laguna that is about 15 or 20 minutes' walk away, and swim there. Personally, I prefer a more organized place like Xel-Ha.

There is a small entrance fee, less than a dollar. You can change there, there is a small restaurant. Everybody says to go early before the crowds, you will see more fish, the water will be clearer. You can also rent equipment, but we used the equipment we had rented in Akumal. It was just fantastic, again, warm, crystal-clear water full of nice and friendly fish. We even saw a big ray at the bottom. The lagoon is not very deep, you can go all around in the volcanic rocks, where some fish loiter and stare at you as you intrude. You are not allowed to go near the sea entrance. At some places visibility was not good, due probably to the mixing of salt and fresh water. You will hear a sort of clicking noise, made not by a motorboat, but by fish called grunts.

It was getting toward the end of the day, the sun was setting, we had a flash storm, five minutes of water. We hurried back the eight kilometers to Akumal. Night comes quickly, and it was well past dark when we reached our room.

DAY SEVEN

We left Akumal around 8 a.m. without breakfast, just some cookies. It was cool outside. The sun was not too strong.

We steered in the direction of Tulum. About 100 meters just past the entrance for Xel-Ha, where we went the previous day, we stopped at the Xel-ha ruins. Though they are not the biggest ruins of the peninsula, they have the advantage of not being much frequented. The caretaker was very nice. He lives in the same manner as the Maya have lived for hundreds of years, in an oval, whitewashed house with thatched roof.

The ruins are divided into two areas. The caretaker will orient you and watch your bicycle. This was our first real contact with the jungle. I am always checking for snakes everywhere. Interestingly, some of the structures have paintings on the walls. The cenote is so large that in fact it looks like a lake. I was surprised to see mangrove vegetation so far inland. The caretaker told us that the water was in fact salty. Probably this cenote, two-and-a-half kilometers from the coast, is connected to it by an underground watercourse.

As we returned to the road, Natalie saw a big branch on the pavement. I had a little more experience of the tropics, and knew it was a snake—about 1.75 meters long, taking a little sunbath. It was green, the color of grass, with some yellow dots. When we approached, it looked at us, stuck out its ess-shaped tongue, then whoosh, it snaked off into the jungle. Natalie, too, whooshed off. At the entrance, the caretaker asked if it was a green snake. He told us there are many of them, they are not poisonous, and do not attack.

We headed for Tulum. There is a small military airport nearby, which is used more as a base for planes spotting forest fires than for anything else.

At the intersection for the side road to the Tulum ruins is the moderately priced Crucero motel. Stop there if you're bushed, though it's right beside the road. And there are more accommodations on the road to Punta Allen, which is paved for a certain distance. Many years ago I stayed in the area, at a place which the owners did nothing to keep clean. There was a mountain of sand on my balcony, all sorts of strange animals, rusted faucets. You should look before you check in. But the beaches are very nice. The beachfront Chac Mool cabañas are recommended. You can stay for about $10 per person, or you can even camp out.

We had our breakfast in a sort of diner at the Motel Crucero, then visited the Tulum ruins, which are, in my opinion, a must. The site, a fortress, is impressive, fantastic. When it was discovered by the Spanish, it was painted in all colors. You can go to the top of the major pyramid for a commanding view of the site and the jungle around it, and the sea in front. I suggest a guided tour to appreciate your visit more.

From Tulum,, if you like, you can go to Cobá, ruins 40 kilometers inland over a flat road. As we were headed to Belize, we decided to continue south, and because of the time we had taken at the ruins, and the unbroken scrub vegetation along the flat road, which now turned inland from the coast, we took a bus. We waited about an hour and a half, two full buses passed us up, but this was no great problem. It was very easy to get our bikes aboard the bus that finally pulled over.

If you are a purist and continue on bicycle, you can find accommodations in Felipe Carrillo Puerto, 95 kilometers south of Tulum. An alternative is to get off the bus at Limones, and continue south and then east for 91 kilometers to Chetumal, along the inland sea called Laguna Bacalar. We went all the way to Chetumal. For two people, including two bicycles, it cost about $17. This worked out to about $5 per person and $3 per bicycle.

The bus terminal in Chetumal looks more like an airport than anything else. There are marble floors, automatic doors, air conditioning, control tower, waiting rooms, departure gates, loudspeaker announcements. And those Mexican drivers, on the smooth, straight roads, act like pilots.

What struck us in Chetumal was that the people are very attractive, especially women, due, perhaps, to their genetic mixture. They are also very kind. We arrived as the sun was setting. One thing bothered us at first. At each intersection were two or three policemen. Well, it's the regional capital, and the heavy police presence did not turn out to be any cause for concern. Because the city looked very quiet, in all ways. Probably, the government just wanted to create jobs.

You can choose hotels according to your budget. We looked at a few, and stayed at the Caribe Princess. It cost about $20 for two. It was clean, air-conditioned, and okay, nothing special, but well located. A couple of floors of additional rooms were under construction, or perhaps they had stopped building the hotel early. Our room was quiet. When we arrived, we asked where to leave our bicycles. They said to come behind the desk, and we chained them there, to the stairway. You can also try the Hotel Real Azteca, but check to see that they give you a quiet room.

We ate in a pizzeria near the hotel, they had a good choice of wine. When we were walking after dinner, we saw a big, old American car, from the seventies. It made quite a lot of noise—putt-putt-putt—and was full of black people, at least ten. We looked at the plates, it was from Belize. That was my first contact with Belize, and, quite frankly, it scared me a little bit, the people looked a little bit threatening. We were to realize later, after a few minutes in Belize, that those big old broken-down cars are full of friendly people.

DAY EIGHT

We left Chetumal after riding around a bit on bicycle. We rode along the Boulevard de la Bahía, looking at the piers and the fishermen. The city is quiet, with a nice seafront, though not good for swimming. If you want to swim, you have to go at least ten kilometers by bicycle.

Then we took the road to Belize. From Chetumal along Highway 186 to the turnoff for Belize is about six kilometers, with some mild grades. One funny thing is that there is a cycling path along the highway. Traffic was moderate, but we were very safe.

From the crossroads for the road to Belize, the land is flat, and farmed with corn. But for a few palms, it could be one of the northern plains states of the United States. There is hardly any traffic.

If you are planning to return through Mexico, it would be a good idea to get a spare tourist card before you leave home. They don't always have these documents on hand at the border, or, at least, they hesitate about finding them, perhaps to see if you will offer a small bribe. When we came back, the tourist cards suddenly appeared, after a few minutes of sweat. Going out of Mexico was no problem.

You cross a bridge over the jungle-lined River Hondo to Santa Elena. We were quite excited about being in Belize. There was a small roadside sentry box, and in it, a black guy with mirror sunglasses, boots in the air. He looked at Natalie and said, "Hey, mon, where you want to go?" Formalities were quite simple, they took about fifteen minutes. It was lucky that we arrived just before a bus full of Mexicans with paper problems. Our bicycle serial numbers were noted in our passports.

At the border, a lot of people ask you to change money. They give an honest rate, two Belizean dollars for one U.S. dollar. We found it fast and easy.

177

Everything looked very clean. It's funny to see all those houses on stilts, even inland, the coastal architecture that takes into account floods carried throughout the country. I suppose that snakes can't get up to a house that's in the air. There's also more of a breeze when you live several meters up, and you're away from the humidity near the ground. Everybody keeps the grass in front of their house neatly cut, like English gardens.

The land is very green, it turned out to be this way all over the country. Crops grow well. There are some rolling hills, but mostly, in the north, the land is flat. Frankly, the human geography is more interesting. People are friendly, everybody waves at you. It smells of happiness.

About five kilometers from the border there is a nice place to swim for a small fee, at a lake, the Four Miles Lagoon, on the left.

We arrived in Corozal, about ten miles from the border, just after a refreshing ten-minute tropical storm—the time it takes to get out your raincoat out and put it back. The people in Corozal were very friendly. But there is something that seems out of place at first. The townspeople are Mestizos, Mayas, and blacks. But the black people look just like they belong in Harlem, with their ghetto blasters, roller skates, their Coke t-shirts, woolen hats, and mirror glasses. But that's just an appearance. They are very friendly, they speak differently, and you feel no racial tension.

We rode along the waterfront, and stopped for lunch at a very nice hotel, Tony's Inn. It was $10 for two, including tip, for a nice chicken dish. The landscaped gardens are lovely. We bought our map of Belize here, and continued on our way.

We found that although the map indicates one main road, we often came to unmarked intersections, with paved roads leading off in various directions. There is always a house, so you might as well ask for the right way. Otherwise, you could continue for a few kilometers, until you find the road surface turning to gravel, and figure that you've taken the wrong turn.

The main road is paved all the way, through the villages of San Francisco, Louisville, Buena Vista, San Roman, and Santa Clara. All are small places with a few shops, some are bigger than others. You pass through sugar-cane fields in the hilly landscape, with great big clouds overhead, the sky is huge. Every time you come to a small rise you can see for quite a distance how things lie along the road.

Between Buena Vista and Santa Clara, Natalie had a small problem. There was some mud on the road, brought by trucks coming from the fields, and some got stuck between the fender and the wheels. So we stopped, and within five seconds, a guy came walking by with some tools in a bag; a little girl ran out of a Mayan hut with two bicycle wrenches; and a guy repairing his car by the roadside offered us some tools as well. So I would say that if you have a problem in Belize, help might not be far away.

We stopped here and there, having a soft drink, chatting to people. From Louisville to Orange Walk there were just trucks carrying sugar cane, all sorts of trucks, old British army trucks, Leylands, Bedfords. It was harvest time. All were heading to the mill just past Orange Walk. Traffic got heavier and heavier. All those trucks, and tractors, passed us very slowly. Drivers waved, it was obvious they were being very careful.

We arrived at about 5 p.m. in Orange Walk. You will see first a small floating bridge off to your left, on the road that crosses the New River. You enter what looks like a wild west town, with wooden storefronts, and the horse-drawn carts of Mennonites.

We stayed at Barron's Hotel. If it is full, go back to the Chula Vista, which is just north of town along the highway. The other accommodations in town are nothing to attract you. Barron's is a cyclist's heaven, quite modest in appearance, with a nice pool in the parking lot, with water that smells chlorinated. The rooms are clean, and afford a nice view over the village.

In one of the general stores, we asked for a restaurant, they sent us to the San Francisco restaurant. Don't go there. We arrived at the door, and turned back. Then we took the advice of our hotel manager. We went across from our hotel to the Orange Walk Restaurant, run by recent immigrants from Hong Kong. We had a big platter of curried shrimp, it was very good, I just hoped I wouldn't get sick from it. In the end, I wasn't, and I only worried, when I went to bed, about outlaws and bank robberies. We did a good 70 kilometers during the day.

One interesting thing about Orange Walk: they mention in some guides that Orange Walk was an internationally known cannabis center. In fact, I saw some suspect tourists at Barron's Hotel. Probably, it had to do with the declining price of sugar cane. One of the two sugar mills had closed. So instead of cane, they grew cannabis.

DAY NINE

We left Orange Walk very early in the morning. This was supposed to be a very long day, by the Northern Highway, nearly 60 miles, or 95 kilometers. It turned out otherwise.

If you come this way, I suggest you leave with the sun to get a start against the heat. Take a good supply of food and water. Replenishments are hardly available for a good part of this route. Pick up oranges and the like the night before.

A little bit past Orange Walk, near Chan Pine Ridge village, is the sugar mill, the mecca of all those trucks we had been passing. Seeing them all turn onto a side road, we decided to follow them. All the drivers looked strangely at us—maybe they thought we had some sugar cane in our packs. The line of trucks was more than a mile long. We had a look at the operation. A big crane grabbed and piled up the sugar cane. Three great chimneys poured forth a dense, black smoke. All along the highway there had been the sweet smell of cane. And at the mill it was even stronger. At this time of year, the factory ran around the clock.

Back on the highway, we came to the New River, the water of which didn't look very nice. It was a jungly, tropical river. I think there are some crocodiles there. It's a good place to stop for a soft drink, though, at the adjacent Jim's Cool Pool. It was still quite early in the morning.

We crossed the toll bridge, which for us was free. And beyond was a new road, called the New Northern Highway. We didn't understand that it was the Old Northern Highway that passes the Altun Ha ruins, where we wanted to stop. We didn't even see the sign for the intersection. We just went ahead, pedalling and pedalling for about three hours through a nowhere landscape, flat, logged out, empty of people, all uninteresting flat countryside covered with brush, and an occasional cattle pasture.

The road was straight, and there were big metal poles planted alongside, every three to four hundred meters. Later we learned that those metal poles were put there to prevent airplanes landing at night on that very good runway, and taking controlled substances out to the States.

Strangely, we kept coming along signs for villages, population 200 souls or whatever. Welcome to X. You see nothing, not even a house. Then, several miles later, you see "Good Bye, come again." There were several phantom villages like that. Most likely, there are houses off to the side, down some path or bumpy road, along some river or lagoon that provided the only transport until the New Northern Highway was pushed through the village outskirts.

About 30 kilometers past the toll bridge there is a restaurant on the left. It is the only place to stop before you get to the vicinity of Belize City.

At Biscayne, there are at least some houses scattered here and there along the road. Past Sand Hill, the road is a little bit bumpy, but it's not too bad. The bumps continue every now and then to Ladyville.

I didn't know why it's called Ladyville. Perhaps this is the reason: there is a place called Raul's Rose Garden. We went there for a soft drink, but it is, in fact, a lady ville.

If you get to Ladyville by 5 p.m., I would suggest that you not continue to Belize City. There is a hotel, the International Hotel, by the airport. It looks clean. Or, you can stay at Raul's Rose Garden, with proper preventive measures.

If was still mid-afternoon when we passed through, however.

If you have more time, take the Maskall road after the New River bridge, and stop at Altun Ha. Don't miss the turnoff, the way we did. The winding Old Northern Highway is probably more interesting for cycling than the flat, straight road we went on, though in poor condition, and somewhat longer. We saved about 15 kilometers by unintentionally taking the new road.

Past Ladyville, the road is very well maintained, in fact, it looks like a road in England, with reflectors, lined by trees, and with a river flowing alongside. We reached Belize City, and traffic was not at all heavy—it was a Sunday afternoon.

Well, the place is interesting, in its way, peculiar, with so many houses on stilts crowded upon each other, looking as if they're about to fall down. You have very nice views when you arrive by boat, or when you are on the Swing Bridge and look up and down Haulover Creek. There is an interest from an architectural point of view, a few old buildings that remind you of a certain era. You don't expect this kind of town, after coming through so much emptiness.

Natalie was very surprised in Belize City. In fact, she is a specialist in microbiology. She looked very carefully at the open drainage, she lay down and looked closely, and saw a big piece of - - - - passing in the dark, troubled water, then she looked at me and realized that it was sewage out there in the open. I suspect it is not good to swim off Belize City.

All around Belize City we found people very helpful and friendly. Only in the downtown area, near the market, and the Swing Bridge, don't talk to strangers. There are only hustlers, as my guidebook had warned us, with dope for sale, boat rides to offer, sick relatives in need, and a thousand other stories in aid of parting you from your money. They are not dangerous, at least, I don't think they are. But they are part of a small cultural shock.

As for all those old cars, I found the explanation in Belize City. There is a very high tax on new cars. The older the car, the lower the tax, so mostly old cars are imported. You have the feeling of being in the same place ten or fifteen years ago. In Orange Walk, you have the feeling you are fifty years early.

We turned to the Fort George Hotel for dinner when we arrived. We left our bicycles in the lobby, we were full of mud, but no problem. They were not unused to odd visitors. We had a very good meal in a fully air conditioned dining room. But we didn't stay there for the night at $96 for a very ordinary room. Nor would I suggest that you spend a night in Belize City. I don't think it is unsafe to stay in Belize City, I just don't see any interest in doing so. It's worth a quarter-day, maybe.

If you end up spending the night in Belize City, I would suggest that you select carefully. Some hotels are quite high-priced, and are not good value, but they're secure, at least, once you're inside. A fellow called Chocolate organizes boat trips from a slip on the north side of Haulover Creek, near the Swing Bridge, including some to lagoons near Belize City for bird watching. If we had more time, we would have taken that tour. Chocolate has a store on Caye Caulker where you can ask about his trips. They're supposed to be fantastic.

We went to the Shell station near the Swing Bridge to look for a boat to Caye Caulker. (There's now a more formal boat terminal nearby.) Usually, they leave at 11 in the morning. But you can find a boat at a later hour. The price will be higher, but it will get you to a caye. We arranged passage on a big speedboat with two motors, for ourselves and our two bicycles. Very easy, very fast.

We arrived after sunset. It cost us $6 per person to go there, and $5 per bicycle. Fair enough, for the bicycles took up half the boat. It's a good thing to leave at night, as there isn't much demand for transport, and there was no problem in getting the bikes aboard the boat.

Don't stay in the first hotel you come across, the Martinez. Go down the island, to the south. The Tropical Paradise itself is the best hotel, clean and pleasant. Deisy's Hotel is good, Hotel Marin and the basic Edith's will also do. Visit all, they are quite near each other, and make your choice. You can always bargain a little bit.

The only good restaurant, in my opinion, is at the Tropical Paradise. We had a lobster plate there. It was $4, not gourmet food, but never in my life have I eaten such fresh lobster so cheaply.

The roads on the island are quite limited, and easy to drive on, despite the sand, even for Natalie on her regular touring bike. But the place is small, so you'll end up walking. Make sure you secure your bike well, because everybody on the island knows that you have one.

DAY TEN

This day was quite easy, in fact, relaxed. We met people from Quebec, some of whom had already been on Caye Caulker for a few months, and looked more like indigenous people than the natives. In fact, they called it Gilligan's Island.

We went snorkeling along the barrier reef, the longest in the hemisphere. You can rent equipment very cheaply, and find others to share a boat. We were with Germans, Belgians, and one native of the island. The fish there are very, very nice. We made three dives. There is interesting coral. We only did snorkeling. Mostly, we were just in water to our chests. One time, I saw Natalie going at the speed of a boat, I realized she saw something, later we figured it was a nurse shark, which is not dangerous, only surprising, because there is a lot of food. I'm glad that I didn't see it. If you go fishing, be very careful, never bring dead fish as bait.

That's all for that day, only small emotions.

DAY ELEVEN

We were supposed to take a scuba trip. Due to strong wind and bad weather, the trip was cancelled quite early in the morning, and we left around 7 a.m. on one of the first boats for Belize City.

If you leave Caye Caulker early, you will get a good price. If you have to leave later, you will have to bargain. All the boat drivers have the same story, that gasoline is expensive. In fact, from what I know of speedboats, it would cost no more than $10 in fuel for a trip like that.

We departed Belize City right off. It is one good bicycling day from Belize City to Belmopan, the capital, a distance of 80 kilometers. When you leave, you are in swamps, for about 40 kilometers you see nothing but swamps and mangrove trees on the left and on the right, sometimes near a lagoon you see a lot of birds. The road is not heavily trafficked. Even in Belize City traffic was light.

It was easy going, a straight road. We rode most of the way, and then we flagged down a bus. In 30 minutes we had done the last 30 kilometers.

I have to tell you that it is quite easy to take a bus in Belize. They have racks on top. You put up your bicycle yourself. They give you all the time you need to attach them, they are not in a rush. And the bus just continues. The pace is very easy, people are very cool, and you don't have to worry about anything. In all of Belize, we never felt threatened, and were not afraid of being robbed. We felt that most of the people were very gentle. Of course you have to take care and watch your things. I am told that theft is a problem in Belize City.

From along the road you begin to see Mountain Pine Ridge. It is rolling. About ten miles before Roaring Creek, there is a zoo. You can get there in a few hours from Belize City, it can be your mid-day stop. We met people who visited it. It has all the local species. We wanted to go, but with only a few days remaining, we continued onward. At Roaring Creek, you turn south onto the Southern Highway, which looks much smaller as a road. A left turn again takes you into Belmopan.

When we arrived in Belmopan I didn't feel very well. For my breakfast on Caye Caulker, I had had pancakes and bacon. There are no pigs on the island, and no chickens for the eggs, so something wasn't fresh. I was sick, but not too much.

Because I didn't feel well, we saw the Belmopan Convention Centre, and decided to stay there, thinking, why not take a good hotel when you are sick? And there was a pool. The price is $67 double. I think this was a mistake. There is another hotel called the Circle A, at half the price, that looked like a flower pot in the concrete mass of Belmopan. Though everybody was very kind at the Convention Centre. They let us take our bicycles inside, no problems there. The meals were very good, though I only watched.

In the evening my breakfast went out, and with a good night's sleep, everything was all right the next morning.

DAY TWELVE

I had an easy morning, and a little swim. There were big clouds out, but it didn't look like it was going to be a rainy day. Natalie took the time to write some post cards in the morning. I bought topographical maps at the Ministry of Natural Resources. You can buy these in person in two sheets, on a scale of 1:250,000, by mail, for $12.

We left Belmopan about 10 a.m. We went back on the Western Highway. At Roaring Creek we stopped at the post office. It looked like a normal residential house, with a "post office" sign outside, as if this were a side job. When we left, we looked up to see children waving to us from the second floor, our post cards in their hands. They were written in French, so the kids could not understand, I think. And everybody we wrote to got their cards. Probably this is a normal step in postal sorting in Belize.

From Belmopan, our destination was San Ignacio, or Cayo. That road is very, very nice. It is rolling countryside, you go up and down. It is not striking, it is pleasant. The road is quite easy.

Along the way you see all sorts of churches, nice ranches, cows, horses, and a lot of Mennonites who farm in that area. Some live in the horse-and-buggy era, others, around Spanish Lookout, have big pickup trucks. Take out the palm trees, lower the temperature a little bit, and you are in the middle of the United States, a rich agricultural land. In this distance, you have the Maya Mountains, which look something like the Appalachians.

In the area of Ontario Village, we stopped for a soft drink. It was funny to watch black people playing dominoes. When they put the dominoes on the table they did it with a bang! to impress people around the table. That reminded Natalie of similar scenes in North Carolina, where she had once been biking.

Later on, a man with big mirror glasses was lying down in the middle of the road. I think he just wanted to be cool. When we went by, he jumped up, caught his glasses, and looked at us like he just didn't believe what he was seeing.

About 15 kilometers before Cayo, on the right, there is a sign advertising black coral jewelry and furniture. If you like that sort of thing, stop there. It's also a good place to stop for wine and cheese or beer, at a good price. It was warm and sunny, but just as we stopped, there was a cloudburst. We had company waiting out the storm, and listened to the small machinery in a hut next door.

The turnoff for Maya Mountain Lodge is just before Cayo. It is very nice, but there is no pool. We wanted to swim, so we decided to continue to another hotel, the San Ignacio. You cross the Macal River, and turn left—ask for directions. The town is full of hotels. We found the San Ignacio full. They let us swim anyway. Then we asked for other hotels. They said there were others like the Maya Mountain Lodge on various ranches west of San Ignacio, in the direction in which we were going.

We went to the Windy Hill Cottages on Graceland Ranch, two kilometers out of town on the road to Benque Viejo and the Guatemalan border, and 50 kilometers from Belmopan. They had opened only recently, and were very kind. They treated us more as friends than guests. But their prices were exorbitant. If you have time, which we didn't have, you can compare accommodations. I would suggest that you stay at least three days in this area, in which case it would be worth taking an hour to look at some of the accommodations.

This one had four cottages at the top of a hill, with commanding views of the area. I would have liked to stay another day, for horseback riding and canoeing. It cost us $30 for a clean, Mayan-style cottage, with hot showers, and ceiling fan. The only thing that I didn't like was the opening between the roof and the walls, which could have allowed crawlies to get inside at night. I felt secure about the food, because the wife of the owner worked for the United Nations health and sanitation program for Salvadoran refugees in Belize, who seem to be very numerous. We had encountered some on the road. The meals were fantastic, although a little bit pricey, at

$10 per person for dinner. But it was a good bicycling meal, and I needed that type of meal. Breakfast was very, very good also. The owner, a Texan (his wife was from Belize) told us he had accommodated two French cyclists, coming from Guatemala, before his hotel was open. They camped on the grass.

DAY THIRTEEN

We wanted to go to Benque Viejo, and visit the ruins at Xunantunich. There was rain in the morning between 5 and 8 a.m., a very heavy rain. When we started out it was cloudy, but we didn't have any more rain, until we came back at night.

After a good breakfast, we started out. It was not fast on that road, it took about one hour to get to Benque Viejo. It was unpaved, and uphill. For people there, in a country that is mostly flat, it is a very big hill. For us, it was a normal, small hill, no problem on our bikes. There is little traffic, but there are buses, so don't worry, if you have any problem, there is somebody to take you on. And you have nice views all around of rolling ranch land.

We passed several other cottage-ranch hotels. A little bit past the Windy Hill Cottages is the entrance road for the Chaa Creek Cottages. Then there is one called El Indio Suizo. They have room for about 20 people, overlooking the Mopan River. It's a relaxing, exotic environment.

Along that road we saw a column of young men in battle dress. They were British soldiers. The British have a base, in case of an invasion from Guatemala, which has on and off pressed its claim to Belize. Now it seems settled that Guatemala will abandon its claim. Also, there is some guerrilla activity, not in Belize, but in the northern part of the Peten department in Guatemala. The guerrillas don't operate on the Belizean side because they have absolutely no interest in facing the British army. Belize is hardly a revolutionary place. Most of the people, from what I have seen, although they are not rich, live well enough.

A little bit before Benque Viejo, a ferry crosses to the road to the Mayan ruins of Xunantunich. The man on duty said the river was too high, due to recent rains, to operate the free cable ferry, which takes vehicles. But, conveniently, he operated his own private dugout, and took people across one by one.

If you can get across on the ferry, the road is quite negotiable on a mountain bicycle for the mile to the ruins, or you can walk. It's pleasant, slightly uphill, through rain forest. Just near the ferry, on the left, coming from San Ignacio, is a small store. It was operated by an American when I was through. You might be able to leave your bicycle there; or at the health center nearby, at Succotz.

By the ferry, we ran into a group of churchy people, which in itself was not surprising, for you see churches of various sects and missionaries in all of the more pleasant areas of Latin America. They asked us, rather aggressively, what we were doing in life, what was our religion. It was surprising. There were no people at the boat, so they said ah, those people are very lazy. It was quite a surprise. They were in a truck, on which was written, Church of Jesus Christ. Later on, at home, I saw an article about the Church of Jesus Christ Christian, which turned out to be a whites-only, ultra-right organization. What they hoped to accomplish in racially mixed-up Belize I don't know.

We visited Xunantunich, a nice site, and climbed the main pyramid, which is the tallest structure in Belize, except for one at the remote Caracol ruins. We had a good view of all the area. Due to the bad weather of the previous week, there had not been any tourists.

We took our bicycles back at the small store. We came back slowly, and arrived about 4 p.m. With stopping here and there, and speaking to people, it was a full day.

I suggest you continue your visit to Benque Viejo, but stop there. Distances between stopping points on the other side of the border, in Guatemala, are greater, roads are poor, there are accommodations only in Tikal and the Flores area. If you want to go onward, I would suggest that you take buses for part of the way.

DAY FOURTEEN

This was the bad day. I would have liked to stay more in San Ignacio, there are lots of things to see and do. You are very near nature. And there are a lot of accommodations and organized tours. Or you can go out on a mountain bike to Mountain Pine Ridge, where they are numerous caves and waterfalls.

With more time, we could have gone south from Belmopan to Dangriga along the Hummingbird Highway, through the foothills of the Maya Mountains. We could have even gone onward to the Petén department of Guatemala, though the poor roads and limited accommodations, with long distances in between, were not too tempting. Or we could have returned to the cayes, chartered a boat to Chetumal, and then gone on by road.

But we had taken a charter flight to Cancun to save money, and now we had to return. So we went directly back by bus from San Ignacio, all day. I don't want to talk about it too much. It cost about $10 to Chetumal, another $10 to Cancun, including the bicycles. It's very, very long, but the roads are flat, and the buses are good. We left at 8 a.m., and had a good stop in Chetumal, because we had to wait there for a bus with room. We spent three hours, had supper, biked in town, and along the sea. Then we continued to Cancun. It was a long day. But as I have said, the air fare if we had arrived in Cancun and left from Belize would have been exactly double.

In Cancun, due to the lack of time, as we were leaving the next morning, we stayed at Hotel Plaza Caribe, which is opposite the bus station, though, due to an inside court, it is very nice. They have a pool and many other facilities. We arrived at 11 p.m., and they asked about $65 for the room. I met somebody on the plane home who said he stayed there for $40. Well, it was 11 p.m., we wanted to sleep, and they took advantage of us. We got in a swim, anyway. Take your time, if you're not too tired and it's not late, you can bargain, even in nice hotels.

DAY FIFTEEN

It was time to take the plane back. From downtown Cancun, we too a slow ride the long way around, by the road along the whole peninsula, not the direct highway. There are so many hotels, and more being built. There is even a cycling path that starts at the beginning of the hotel zone and runs to the Camino Real. Beyond, you have to be cautious. The place is booming, everything, tourists, workers and construction materials moves by that road. Traffic is lighter after the Sheraton.

We arrived safely at the airport at about 10:30 a.m., went through our usual disassembly procedures, and were back in the cold in a few hours.

12
MORE INFORMATION

HEALTH CONDITIONS

Many public health clinics and travellers clinics have information about vaccinations and preventative measures for travellers to various countries.

Health Information for International Travel, published annually by the U.S. Department of Health and Human Services, Centers for Disease Control, details risks of yellow fever, malaria, typhoid, polio, hepatitis, and several other diseases in various countries, and gives general health information for travel to the tropics. Available from the U.S. Government Printing Office, Washington, D.C. 20402.

For specific, late-breaking information, call the Communicable Disease Hotline of the Centers for Disease Control in Atlanta, at 404-332-4555, or search for their site on the Internet.

GUIDES AND MAPS

Guidebooks for Latin America in English (and French, German and Spanish for that matter) are becoming easier to come by. There are regional guides published by Fodor's and other companies, and country-specific guides published by Passport Press (among others).

It's important to understand that in many cases, the quality of coverage is hit-or-miss, which is not necessarily the fault of the writers. Some of the Fodor's guides contain consistent, hilarious errors in Spanish that can only have been inserted by a supervising editor. Maps in different series have a funny way of agreeing in their mistakes. The same facilities, lavishly described, turn up in competing books, but not on the ground. Let me stop the tirade at this point, and simply advise you to rely on what you see, and hear from other travellers, as well as what you read.

The *South American Handbook and Mexico and Central America Handbook* (Footprint series, Trade & Travel Publications), are more directories and collection of facts than guidebooks, but are reasonably accurate, and are generally the most helpful publications you can use when you can't find a good specific guide.

Passport Press publishes Paul Glassman's Guatemala Guide, Costa Rica Guide and Belize Guide. I've used the first two, and found them excellent, with much information relevant to biking trips—road conditions, accommodations in remote areas, etc. These can be ordered from Box 1346, Champlain, New York 12919. (The editions of these books published by another company were not accurately updated.)

The encyclopedic *Guide to Venezuela* (Armitano) is published in Caracas in English. It was out of print at the time of my trip, but if you go to Venezuela, it's worth checking to see if it has been re-issued.

Chile has good regional map-guide booklets published by the Banco de Osorno. These are widely available within Chile, and can be used even with only a limited command of Spanish.

For Argentina, buy the Automóvil Club Argentino's maps locally. Some local tourist offices publish quite good information in English.

For the Dominican Republic, I used a guidebook published in France. It wasn't comprehensive, or as up-to-date as the South American Handbook.

Of the many, many books on bicycling and bicycle touring, the most complete is *Bike Touring: The Sierra Club Guide to Outings on Wheels*, by Raymond Bridge. The magazines *Bicycling* and *Bicycle Rider* contain useful information for bicycle travel, including articles on touring in various countries.

Most general bookstores do not carry more than a limited lineup of travel books; book superstores, specialized travel bookstores, and online sites are a better bet.

In the United States and Canada, some of the best available maps of Latin American countries are those published by ITMB (P. O. Box Box 2290, Vancouver, B.C. V6B 3W5 Canada). These contain a wealth of topographical and even historical information, so much so that it's sometimes difficult to decipher everything; but use your magnifying glass if you have to. In some cases, these maps are more useful than guidebooks.

Discover Great Travel with PASSPORT PRESS

NICARAGUA GUIDE by Paul Glassman
0-930016-22-X $19.95
"Paul Glassman, one of the best-known writers on Central America, has [re-launched] his own series. This delightful guide emphasizes the beauty of Nicaragua's untouched tropical jungles, sentinel volcanoes, colonial cities and Pacific beaches."
Library Journal

HONDURAS AND THE BAY ISLANDS by Paul Glassman and J. P. Panet   0-930016-23-8 $15.95
Adventure where few have gone before!
"As accurate as any you will find"
The Guide to Travel Guides

MONTREAL AND THE CASINO by Jack Levesque and Zack Lewis   0-930016-21-1 $12.95
The world's greatest casino is within a day's drive of 100 million people. Fame and fortune are possibilities. The fun is guaranteed! Includes the most concise guide to this 24-hour city of joie de vivre, bargains, and endless excitement.

GUATEMALA GUIDE by Paul Glassman
0-930016-26-2 $16.95
The classic that launched a whole generation of travel guides.
"Full of useful information . . .thoroughly explores the territory and subject." *Booklist*

BELIZE GUIDE by Paul Glassman
0-930016-25-4 $14.95
Diving, rain forest, the longest reef in the hemisphere, Mayan ruins, and a reggae beat. Been there yet?
"*Belize Guide* is *the* book you need. Don't leave home without it!"   *International Travel News*

COSTA RICA GUIDE by Paul Glassman
0-930016-24-6 $19.95
Paradise or promo? Glassman guides you through rain forest, fishing, diving, and scenic wonders, and around the hype.
"If you have to choose one guidebook, [choose] Glassman's."
Travel and Leisure

www.ingramcontent.com/pod-product-compliance
Lightning Source LLC
Chambersburg PA
CBHW052000090426
42741CB00008B/1482